P/O NO.
ACCESSION NO: K.
SHELFMARK: R EBS/IRE
616.0076

MRCOG PART 1
MCQ REVISION BOOK

David Ireland MD BChir MA MRCOG
Consultant Gynaecological Surgeon
Leicester Royal Infirmary and Leicester General Hospitals.

PASTEST
Dedicated to your success

© 1994 PasTest
Egerton Court
Parkgate Estate
Knutsford
Cheshire WA16 8DX

All rights reserved. No part of this publication may be reproduced, stored in a retrieval system, or transmitted, in any form or by any means, electronic, mechanical, photocopying, recording or otherwise without the prior permission of the copyright owner.

First published 1994
Reprinted 1995
Reprinted 1999

ISBN: 0 906896 91 6

A catalogue record for this book is available from the British Library.

Text prepared by Turner Associates, Congleton, Cheshire.
Printed by Biddles Ltd, Guildford and Kings Lynn.

CONTENTS

INTRODUCTION

This second edition of our MRCOG Part 1 multiple choice book has been extensively modified compared with the first edition. The MCQs have been grouped together by subject area corresponding to the College syllabus and each section is followed by correct answers and valuable teaching notes. Two complete practice exams are then provided which should ideally be taken under exam conditions. The first can be completed towards the beginning of your revision and the second some weeks later. In this way you will be able to identify your weak areas of knowledge in time for further study before the exam.

The Royal College of Obstetricians and Gynaecologists recently published a syllabus and this is summarised:

Anatomy
A comprehensive knowledge of the anatomy of the pelvis, abdomen, thorax, breast, thigh and all the endocrine glands. Anatomical details of bones, joints, muscles, blood vessels, lymphatics, nerve supply and central connections of the above as well as the embryological development, histology and relationships to surrounding structures.

Biochemistry
Detailed knowledge of the metabolism of carbohydrates, fats, proteins, nucleic acids, vitamins, minerals and enzymes. The distribution of chemicals in the body compartments and the composition of intracellular, extracellular fluids and secretions from exocrine and endocrine glands (including placenta and fetus).

Biophysics
Physical principles of ionising irradiation, radioisotopes, X-rays, ultrasound, nuclear magnetic resonance and electrocardiography.

Embryology
Comprehensive knowledge of gametogenesis, fertilisation, organogenesis, the development of the embryo in all body systems, fetal circulation, placental development, amniotic fluid formation and its constituents, including the anatomical and physiological changes in the newborn.

Endocrinology
Comprehensive knowledge of all hormones and humoral agents (both sexes) including their chemistry, formation from precursors, storage, release,

transport, mode of action, regulation and distribution in all body compartments as well as their physiological and pathological activities.

Genetics
Understanding of genetic principles in the mode of inheritance of dominant, recessive and sex-linked disorders, including details of chromosomal disorders, gene identification and principles of cell division.

Immunology
Comprehensive understanding of immune mechanisms, antigen/antibody characteristics and their recognition, including inoculation/vaccination, allergies and anaphylatic reactions.

Microbiology
Comprehensive knowledge of the characteristics, recognition, prevention, eradication and pathological effects of all commonly encountered bacteria, viruses, Rickettsia, fungi, protozoans, parasites and toxins, including an understanding of the principles of infection control.

Pathology
Comprehensive knowledge of general pathological principles including general, local and cellular response to trauma, infection, inflammation, irradiation and disturbances in blood flow, loss of body fluids and neoplasia. Details of common pathological conditions in the body systems.

Pharmacology
Comprehensive knowledge of the chemistry, administration, transport, breakdown, excretion and indications for use, pharmacological effects and complications of commonly used drugs/anaesthetics, in the mother, fetus and neonate.

Physiology
Comprehensive knowledge of general physiology of all body systems with particular reference to conception, the fetus and the neonate. A knowledge is also expected of nutrition, water, electrolyte and acid-base balance as well as ageing and cell biology. Values of normal levels/parameters of common physiological activities should be known.

Statistics and epidemiology
Definition and understanding of commonly used terms and techniques including their applications in clinical research trials.

MCQ EXAMINATION TECHNIQUE

Multiple Choice Questions are the most consistent, reproducible and internally reliable method we have of testing recall of factual knowledge. Yet there is evidence that they are able to test more than simple factual recall; reasoning ability and an understanding of basic facts, principles and concepts can also be assessed. A good MCQ paper will discriminate accurately between candidates on the basis of their knowledge of the topics being tested. It must be emphasised that the most important function of an MCQ paper of the type used in the MRCOG Part 1, is to rank candidates accurately and fairly according to their performance in that paper. Accurate ranking is the key phrase; this means that all MCQ examinations of this type are, in a sense, competitive.

Technique
The safest way to pass MRCOG Part 1 is to know the answers to all of the questions, but it is equally important to be able to transfer this knowledge accurately onto the answer sheet. All too often, candidates suffer through an inability to organise their time, through failure to read the instructions carefully or through failure to read and understand the questions. First of all you must allocate your time with care. There are two examination papers covering the syllabus as outlined in the introduction. In each paper there are 60 questions (each of 5 parts) to be completed in 2 hours; this means 2 minutes per question or 10 questions in 20 minutes. Make sure that you are getting through the exam at least at this pace, or, if possible, a little quicker, thus allowing time at the end for revision and a re-think on some of the items that you have deferred.

You must read the question (both stem and items) carefully. You should be quite clear that you know what you are being asked to do. Once you know this, you should indicate your responses by marking the paper boldly, correctly and clearly. Take great care not to mark the wrong ovals and think very carefully before making a mark on the answer sheet.

Regard each item as being independent of every other item, each refers to a specific quantum of knowledge. The item (or the stem and the item taken together) make up a statement. You are required to indicate whether you regard this statement as 'True' or 'False'. Look only at a single statement when answering, disregard all the other statements presented in the question. They have nothing to do with the item on which you are concentrating.

Sample Answer Card

Royal College of Obstetricians and Gynaecologists
Part 1 Membership Examination – Paper 1

SURNAME (FAMILY NAME) MARSHALL

OTHER NAME(S) SARAH ELIZABETH

Please use HB pencil. Rub out all errors thoroughly.
Mark lozenges like ▬ NOT like ✓ ✗ ⊝

T = True
F = False

CANDIDATE NUMBER

1	8	5	6

IMPORTANT NOTES

1. When you have finished, check that you have NOT left any blanks.

2. Erasures should be left clean, with no smudges where possible. (The document reading machine will accept the darkest response for each item).

	A	B	C	D	E			A	B	C	D	E
1	T F	T F	T F	T F	T F		16	T F	T F	T F	T F	T F
2	T F	T F	T F	T F	T F		17	T F	T F	T F	T F	T F
3	T F	T F	T F	T F	T F		18	T F	T F	T F	T F	T F
4	T F	T F	T F	T F	T F		19	T F	T F	T F	T F	T F
5	T F	T F	T F	T F	T F		20	T F	T F	T F	T F	T F
6	T F	T F	T F	T F	T F		21	T F	T F	T F	T F	T F
7	T F	T F	T F	T F	T F		22	T F	T F	T F	T F	T F
8	T F	T F	T F	T F	T F		23	T F	T F	T F	T F	T F
9	T F	T F	T F	T F	T F		24	T F	T F	T F	T F	T F
10	T F	T F	T F	T F	T F		25	T F	T F	T F	T F	T F
11	T F	T F	T F	T F	T F		26	T F	T F	T F	T F	T F
12	T F	T F	T F	T F	T F		27	T F	T F	T F	T F	T F
13	T F	T F	T F	T F	T F		28	T F	T F	T F	T F	T F
14	T F	T F	T F	T F	T F		29	T F	T F	T F	T F	T F
15	T F	T F	T F	T F	T F		30	T F	T F	T F	T F	T F

CHECK THAT YOU HAVE ANSWERED EVERY ITEM TRUE OR FALSE

KENDATA Data Entry Technology   0703 869922

Sample answer sheet, reproduced by kind permission of the Royal College of Obstetricians and Gynaecologists.

X

Marking your answer sheets

The answer sheet will be read by an automatic document reader, which transfers the information it reads to a computer. It must therefore be filled out in accordance with the instructions. A sample sheet is shown opposite. You must first fill in your name on the answer sheet, and then fill in your examination number. It is critical that this is filled in correctly.

As you go through the questions, you can either mark your answers immediately on the answer sheet, or you can mark them in the question book first, transferring them to the answer sheets at the end. If you adopt the second approach, you must take great care not to run out of time, since you will not be allowed extra time to transfer marks to the answer sheet from the question book. The answer sheet must always be marked neatly and carefully according to the instructions given. Careless marking is probably one of the commonest causes of rejection of answer sheets by the document reader. Although the computer operator will do his best to interpret correctly the answer you intended, and will then correct the sheet accordingly, the procedure introduces a possible new source of error. You are, of course, at liberty to change your mind by erasing your original selection and selecting a new one. In this event, your erasure should be carefully, neatly, and completely carried out.

Try to leave time to go over your answers again before the end, in particular going back over any difficult questions that you wish to think about in more detail. At the same time, you can check that you have marked the answer sheet correctly. However, repeated review of your answers may in the end be counter-productive, since answers that you were originally confident were absolutely correct, often look rather less convincing at a second, third or fourth perusal. In this situation, first thoughts are usually best and too critical a revision might lead you into a state of confusion.

To guess or not to guess

Having read the question you are faced with three possibilities:

1. **You can answer the question.** Good. Answer as you think best. Bear in mind you may still be wrong. In order to make the exam as good a discriminator as possible, questions which everyone answers correctly may be removed from the final marking.

2. **You are not sure of the answer but can use your knowledge and reasoning to work out an answer.** Many of the questions will fall into this category and you may well be able to work out the correct answer.

3. **You have no idea what the answer is.** Because you do not lose a mark for a wrong answer – guess. The removal of negative marks seems a big relief. In fact, everyone has the same advantage. With the negative marking system it was found that the more questions people answered the better they scored, so with the removal of negative marking the people likely to benefit are those who were loathe to guess.

Trust the examiners

Do try to trust the examiners. Accept each question at its face value, and do not look for hidden meanings, catches and ambiguities. MCQs are not designed to trick or confuse you, they are designed to test your knowledge of medicine. Don't look for problems that are not there – the obvious meaning of a statement is the correct one and the one that you should read.

To repeat the four most important points of technique:

1. Read the question carefully and be sure you understand it.
2. Mark your responses clearly, correctly and accurately.
3. Use reasoning to work out answers, but if you do not know the answer and cannot work it out, indicate 'Don't know'.
4. The best way to obtain a good mark is to have as wide a knowledge as possible of the topics being tested in the examination.

Acknowledgements

I would like to thank the following for their useful contributions to this book: Keith Godfrey MBChB MRCOG, Consultant Obstetrician and Gynaecologist, Sunderland District Hospital and Paul Hilton, Consultant Gynaecologist, Royal Victoria Infirmary, Newcastle-upon-Tyne.

DI

RECOMMENDED READING LIST

There is no specific reading list for the Part 1 MRCOG examination, but there is a large number of books covering material for the examination; the candidate must discover for him/herself which texts they find most useful. It is essential not to confuse the mind by reading a subject in unnecessary detail, and often the smaller, concise texts are preferable to large volumes. The MCQ questions in this book have been designed to cover most of the topics which are likely to occur in the examination. Subjects which appear commonly are often represented by more than one question. Having completed the questions in the book, it is suggested that the candidate goes through the text again, noting the topics, especially those which recur. This should help to direct reading and further study. An exhaustive reading list is not supplied but the following texts are recommended by the author.

Basmajian J.V., **Grants's Method of Anatomy,** 11th edition. 1989 Waverly Europe.

De Sweit M et al, **Basic Sciences in Obstetrics and Gynaecology,** 2nd edition. 1992 Churchill Livingstone.

Forsling M.L., **Learning Physiology Through MCQ.** 1988 John Wiley and Sons Ltd.

Ganong W.F., **Review of Medical Physiology,** 16th edition. 1993 Appleton Lange.

Grist N.R. et al, **Diseases of Infection,** 2nd edition. 1993 Oxford University Press.

Grundy H.F., **Lecture Notes on Pharmacology,** 2nd edition. 1990 Blackwell Scientific Publications.

McMinn R.M.H., **Last's Anatomy,** Regional and Applied, 8th edition. 1990 Churchill Livingstone.

Petrie A., **Lecture Notes on Medical Statistics,** 2nd edition. 1987 Blackwell Scientific Publications.

Tindall V.R. et al, **Preparation and Advice for the MRCOG.** 1989 Churchill Livingstone.

Underwood J.C.E., **General and Systematic Pathology.** 1992 Churchill Livingstone.

ANATOMY

Indicate your answers with a tick or cross (True or False) in the box provided. The answers and teaching notes to this section start on page 9.

1. The lymphatic drainage

☐ A of the Fallopian tube is mainly via the para-aortic nodes
☐ B of the cervix includes the obturator nodes
☐ C of the corpus uteri includes the superficial inguinal nodes
☐ D of each side of the vulva does not communicate
☐ E of the middle third of the vagina includes the superficial inguinal nodes

2. The obturator nerve

☐ A is formed from the posterior divisions of the 2nd, 3rd and 4th lumbar nerve roots
☐ B is formed within the substance of psoas major
☐ C supplies sensory branches to both hip and knee joints
☐ D has no skin distribution
☐ E supplies motor fibres to obturator internus

3. The ureter

☐ A crosses superior to the uterine artery in the broad ligament
☐ B derives its sympathetic nerve supply from the 2nd and 3rd lumbar nerve roots
☐ C is widest at the pelvi-ureteric junction
☐ D derives its blood supply entirely from the renal and superior vesical arteries
☐ E crosses the pelvic brim lateral to the sacroiliac joint

4. The ischio-rectal fossae

☐ A lie inferior to the levator ani
☐ B lie lateral to the pudendal canal
☐ C have lateral walls formed in part by the obturator internus fascia
☐ D allow dilatation of the anal canal during defaecation
☐ E are separated from each other by the vagina

1

5. In the lower limb

- ☐ A gluteus maximus is supplied by the superior gluteal nerve
- ☐ B piriformis inserts into the lesser trochanter of the femur
- ☐ C psoas major rotates the femur laterally
- ☐ D psoas minor is inserted into the pectineal line
- ☐ E iliacus rotates the femur medially

6. In the anterior abdominal wall

- ☐ A the rectus abdominis lies posterior to the transverse aponeurosis below the umbilicus
- ☐ B the external oblique muscle originates from the lower eight ribs
- ☐ C the superior epigastric artery lies superficial to the rectus abdominis
- ☐ D the pyramidalis muscle is often absent
- ☐ E the median umbilical ligament lies deep to rectus abdominis

7. The uterus

- ☐ A derives its nerve supply from the superior hypogastric plexus
- ☐ B derives most of its support from the broad ligaments
- ☐ C is retroverted in 15% of women
- ☐ D is completely covered with peritoneum posteriorly
- ☐ E develops from the paramesonephric duct

8. Meckel's diverticulum

- ☐ A is present in 10% of individuals
- ☐ B lies 60-70 cm from the caecum
- ☐ C arises from the jejunum
- ☐ D may contain gastric mucosa
- ☐ E may communicate with the umbilicus

9. **The vagina**

☐ A is lined by columnar epithelium
☐ B is kept moist mainly by secretions from Bartholin's glands
☐ C has its upper end above the pelvic floor
☐ D is surrounded by bulbospongiosus muscle at its introitus
☐ E has lateral walls lying in contact with each other when collapsed

10. **The femoral sheath**

☐ A envelops the femoral nerve
☐ B envelops the femoral artery
☐ C lies medial to the lacunar ligament
☐ D is pierced by the genito-femoral nerve
☐ E is narrowest at its proximal end

11. **In the female urethra**

☐ A the distal end is lined by stratified squamous epithelium
☐ B the intramural smooth muscle consists almost entirely of longitudinal fibres
☐ C the normal length is 6-7 cm
☐ D the intrinsic striated muscle is thicker posteriorly
☐ E the sphincter urethrae is supplied by the genital branch of the genito-femoral nerve

12. **The inguinal ligament**

☐ A forms the floor of the inguinal canal
☐ B is inferior to the deep inguinal ring
☐ C is attached laterally to the anterior inferior iliac spine
☐ D is the lower border of the external oblique aponeurosis
☐ E is superior to the ilio-inguinal nerve

13. The trigone of the bladder

☐ A develops from the urogenital sinus
☐ B lies between the ureteric orifices and the urachus
☐ C is more sensitive than the urethra
☐ D is the least mobile part of the bladder
☐ E is always smooth

14. The pudendal nerve

☐ A innervates the internal sphincter of the rectum
☐ B is sensory to the skin of the labia
☐ C runs in the roof of the ischio-rectal fossa
☐ D arises from the same nerve roots as the nerve to the obturator internus muscle
☐ E is formed at the lower part of the greater sciatic foramen

15. The broad ligament

☐ A contains tissues of mesonephric origin
☐ B has the Fallopian tube in its upper free border
☐ C has the ovarian artery in its lower attached border
☐ D has the ureter passing forwards in its lower attached border
☐ E has the ovarian ligament in its posterior fold

16. The levator ani

☐ A consists of smooth muscle
☐ B plays a part in maintaining the position of the uterus
☐ C is supplied by nerves from the lumbar plexus
☐ D has no sphincteric action in relation to the anal canal
☐ E is attached to the pelvic bones

17. The ureter

☐ A is an abdominal organ in 50% of its length
☐ B is closely related to the infundibulo-pelvic ligament
☐ C receives its main blood supply directly from the aorta
☐ D lies on psoas major
☐ E is adherent to the overlying peritoneum

18. The endometrium

☐ A is supplied with blood by the radial and spiral arteries
☐ B shows subnuclear vacuolation of the glandular epithelial cells before ovulation
☐ C shows tortuous lengthened glands in the secretory phase
☐ D shows declining glandular secretion after the 22nd day of the cycle if pregnancy fails to occur
☐ E divides into a superficial compact and deep spongy layer in the functional zone between the 25th and 28th day of the cycle

19. The anterior pituitary

☐ A is known in part as the pars tuberalis
☐ B produces follicle stimulating hormone
☐ C lies above the optic chiasma
☐ D is controlled by releasing factors produced in the hypothalamus
☐ E produces vasopressin

20. The cervix

☐ A undergoes cyclical changes during the menstrual cycle
☐ B loses its lining during menstruation
☐ C has columnar epithelium lining the canal
☐ D produces a thick scanty discharge at ovulation
☐ E has the same proportion of muscle in its wall as the corpus uteri

21. The female breast

- ☐ A is made up of 30-40 units of glandular tissue
- ☐ B overlies pectoralis major and serratus anterior
- ☐ C is connected to true skin by ligaments of Cooper
- ☐ D lymphatics drain to axillary nodes
- ☐ E receives a parasympathetic innervation

22. The femoral nerve supplies

- ☐ A gluteus minimus
- ☐ B rectus femoris
- ☐ C vastus medialis
- ☐ D iliacus
- ☐ E pectineus

23. The long saphenous vein

- ☐ A drains the medial side of leg between tibia and tendo-calcaneous
- ☐ B communicates with the deep veins of the calf
- ☐ C passes behind the medial malleolus
- ☐ D receives the deep external pudendal vein
- ☐ E drains into the femoral vein

24. The sciatic nerve

- ☐ A divides into tibial (medial popliteal) and common peroneal (lateral popliteal) at a variable level in the lower limb
- ☐ B lies under cover of gluteus maximus midway between greater trochanter and ischial tuberosity
- ☐ C is derived from the anterior rami of the 4th and 5th lumbar and 1st, 2nd and 3rd sacral nerves
- ☐ D supplies the gluteal muscles
- ☐ E is the main nerve supplying the adductor magnus

25. The uterine artery

☐ A is a branch of the internal iliac artery
☐ B passes below the ureter in the broad ligament
☐ C does not supply the cervix
☐ D eventually forms an anastomosis with the tubal branch of the ovary artery
☐ E directly supplies the round ligament

26. The labia minora

☐ A contain nerve endings similar to the labia majora
☐ B are derived from the same embryological structure as the labia majora
☐ C have lymphatic drainage to the superficial and deep inguinal nodes
☐ D contain sebaceous glands
☐ E have epithelium which is a mucous membrane on both medial and lateral sides

27. The Mullerian duct

☐ A develops medial to the Wolffian duct
☐ B is also known as the mesonephric duct
☐ C starts to form at 6 weeks of embryonic life
☐ D starts to disappear at 8-9 weeks in the male
☐ E opens into the urogenital sinus in the female

28. The female pelvis differs from the male in the following features:

☐ A all diameters in the male are greater than in the female
☐ B the ischium is relatively longer in the male
☐ C the sacral promontory is more prominent in the male
☐ D the female pubic arch is more acute in the female
☐ E the distance between the acetabulum and the symphysis is greater in the female

29. The pelvic splanchnic nerves

☐ A are also known as the nervi erigentes
☐ B are sympathetic nerves
☐ C arise from S1, 2, 3
☐ D control the muscular walls of the bladder
☐ E carry afferent pain fibres from the pelvis

30. The coeliac trunk

☐ A arises from the aorta
☐ B is 4-5 cm long
☐ C supplies the liver, pancreas and spleen
☐ D has four branches
☐ E gives rise to the superior mesenteric artery

31. The following statements relating to the inguinal canal are correct:

☐ A it contains the round ligament
☐ B the anterior wall is composed mainly of the external oblique aponeurosis
☐ C the posterior wall is formed by the internal oblique muscle
☐ D the deep inguinal ring is superior to the inguinal ligament
☐ E the superficial inguinal ring has a long bony base (the pubic crest)

32. The femoral sheath

☐ A envelops the femoral nerve
☐ B envelops the femoral artery
☐ C lies lateral to the lacunar ligament
☐ D is pierced by a branch of the genitofemoral nerve
☐ E is narrowest at its proximal end

ANSWERS AND TEACHING NOTES : ANATOMY

1. **A B C**

    Lymph from the Fallopian tube drains along the ovarian artery to the para-aortic nodes. The corpus or body of the uterus drains mainly to the internal, external and common iliac nodes. Some channels pass along the round ligaments to the superficial inguinal nodes and others with the ovarian vessels to para-aortic nodes. Drainage of the cervix also includes the obturator nodes. The vagina drains in its upper two thirds to the internal and external iliac nodes and in the lower one third to the upper superficial inguinal nodes. The vulvar drainage of lymph is both ipsilateral and contralateral to the inguinal, internal iliac nodes and femoral nodes of the superficial and deep groups.

2. **B C**

    The obturator nerve is formed within the psoas muscle from the anterior divisions of the 2nd, 3rd and 4th lumbar nerves. It descends medial to psoas and runs along the lateral pelvic wall to the obturator groove through which it passes to reach the thigh; in the thigh it divides into anterior and posterior branches. The anterior division provides a sensory branch to the hip joint and a cutaneous branch to the medial side of the thigh. The posterior division supplies an articular branch to the knee joint and a muscular motor branch to obturator externus and adductor magnus. The anterior division has muscular branches to gracilis, adductor brevis and adductor longus.

3. **B**

    The ureter is widest at its dilated upper end, the renal pelvis, which may contain a volume of 8 ml. The narrowest calibre is found at the pelvi-ureteric junction, where it crosses the pelvic brim and at its termination in the bladder mucosa. The ureter passes down the psoas muscle and crosses the genitofemoral nerve. It leaves the psoas muscle at the bifurcation of the common iliac artery, over the sacro-iliac joint and passes into the pelvis. The ureter then descends on the pelvic wall to the ischial spine before turning forwards and medially under the roof of the broad ligament. Here it is crossed superiorly by the uterine artery and lies in close relation with the lateral fornix of the vagina just before entering the bladder. Blood supply is provided by a longitudinal anastomosis between the renal, ovarian, common iliac and inferior vesical arteries. Sympathetic nerve supply is derived from L1 to L3.

4. **A C D**

    The ischio-rectal fossae are wedge-shaped spaces, the bases being inferior between the ischium and the anal canal. Supero-medially is levator ani attached to obturator fascia above and external anal sphincter below. Laterally the boundaries are fascial on obturator internus and inferiorly by perineal skin. The two fossae communicate with each other round the anal canal and are separated by the anococcygeal body, the anal canal and the perineal body, not by the vagina. The internal pudendal nerves and vessels lie in the lateral walls of the fossae within a sheath. The fossae are filled with soft fat forming a dead space into which the anal canal can expand during defaecation.

5. **D E**

    Gluteus maximus, the prominent muscle of the buttock, is a powerful lateral rotator and extensor at the hip joint and acting through the iliotibial tract, it extends and stabilises the knee joint and is supplied by the inferior gluteal nerve. Piriformis arises inside the pelvis from the anterior surface of the sacrum and passes laterally out of the greater sciatic foramen to be attached to the upper border of the greater trochanter of the femur. Psoas major arises from the five intervertebral discs above lumbar vertebrae and adjacent vertebral bodies and lumbar transverse processes; it is inserted into the lesser trochanter of the femur and flexes and medially rotates the femur at the hip. Psoas minor is a slender muscle lying on the surface of psoas major which arises from the intervertebral disc above the 1st lumbar vertebra and is attached to the arcuate line and iliopectineal eminence. Iliacus is attached to the upper two thirds of the hollow of the iliac fossa; it forms a common tendon with psoas attaching to the lesser trochanter and its function is therefore similar i.e. flexion and medial rotation.

6. **A B D E**

    Laterally the anterior abdominal wall consists of three separate sheet-like layers of muscle, an outer external oblique and intermediate internal oblique and an inner transversalis abdominis. Anteriorly they become aponeurotic, fuse and form the sheath around the rectus abdominis. Above the umbilicus the internal oblique aponeurosis splits to invest the rectus muscle and is reinforced anteriorly by the external oblique and posteriorly by the transversus abdominis. External oblique originates from the outer surfaces of the lower eight ribs. The superior epigastric artery and the inferior epigastric artery with which it anastomoses both lie deep to the rectus abdominis. The obliterated umbilical artery, known in the adult as the lateral umbilical ligament passes obliquely across the posterior wall of the inguinal canal, medial to the inferior epigastric artery. The pyramidalis muscle arises from the pubic crest between the rectus abdominis and its sheath and converges with its fellow into the linea alba an inch or so above its origin; it is frequently absent.

7. **C D E**
    The cranial end of the paramesonephric duct in the female persists and opens directly into the peritoneal cavity; it becomes the uterine tube. The more caudal portions of the two ducts cross medial to the mesonephric ducts and fuse together to form the definitive uterus and upper vagina. Peritoneum covers the majority of the uterus posteriorly as it covers the fundus, body and supravaginal part of the cervix also passing onto the posterior wall of the vagina. The uterus is supported and stabilised by the parametrial ligaments: the uterosacrals, the lateral cervical or cardinal ligaments and pubocervical ligaments. The nerves of the uterus are branches from the inferior hypogastric plexus. The uterus fails to acquire an anteverted position in some 15% of women.

8. **B D E**
    Meckel's diverticulum is a vestige of the vitello-intestinal duct which may persist in 2-3% of the population. It is usually found on the antemesenteric border of the ileum, within 75 cm of the ileo-caecal junction. Its length may vary from little more than a dimple on the bowel wall connected to the umbilicus by a fibrous band, to being patent throughout its length, to communicate with the umbilicus. It may contain gastric, colonic, hepatic or pancreatic tissues which may present with ulcerative symptoms.

9. **C D**
    The vagina is lined by stratified squamous epithelium. Its anterior and posterior walls (not the lateral walls) are normally in contact except at its upper end into which projects the cervix surrounded by a deep sulcus, the fornix. At its upper end it projects above the pelvic floor into the peritoneal cavity. The upper part of the vagina is clasped by the pelvic floor fibres that loop around behind it. The U-shaped sling so formed is named the pubovaginalis (sphincter vaginae). A perineal sphincter (bulbospongiosus) surrounds its outlet. Vaginal lubrication

is provided largely by mucus secreted by the cervix but also during sexual arousal by secretions from Bartholin's glands.

10. **B D**

As the femoral artery and vein pass beneath the inguinal ligament, they draw around themselves a funnel-shaped prolongation of the extraperitoneal fascia, transversalis fascia in front and fascia iliaca behind, known as the femoral sheath. The lacunar or Gimbernat's ligament lies medial to the sheath and the femoral nerve lateral. The genito-femoral nerve is formed within the substance of psoas major from L1 and L2 roots; it divides into its genital and femoral branches above the inguinal ligament. The former pierces transversalis fascia to enter the spermatic cord and the latter passes down in front of the femoral artery, piercing the femoral sheath to supply the skin of the thigh below the middle of the inguinal ligament.

11. **A B**

The female urethra is 3-5 cm in length; it is lined proximally by transitional epithelium continuous with the bladder and distally by squamous epithelium continuous with the introital skin. The exact level of the squamo-transitional junction may vary, in particular with oestrogen status. The intrinsic urethral smooth muscle is orientated largely longitudinally or obliquely and has little or no sphincteric activity. The intrinsic striated muscle (the rhabdosphincter urethrae) is maximal in bulk in mid-urethra anteriorly, thinning laterally and being almost totally deficient posteriorly. Its somatic supply from S2, 3 and 4 has recently been shown to travel in the nervi erigentes, although many traditional texts suggest it comes from the pudendal nerve.

12. **A B D**

The inguinal (Poupart's) ligament extends from the anterior superior iliac spine to the pubic tubercle and is the free lower border of the external oblique aponeurosis. It is rolled inwards inferiorly into a gutter which forms the floor of the inguinal canal, from the deep to the superficial inguinal rings. The ilio-inguinal nerve in the abdomen lies in the neurovascular plane between transversus abdominis and the internal oblique. It pierces the lower fibres of internal oblique to emerge on the round ligament to pass through the superficial ring; it thus lies above the ligament.

13.   **D E**
The trigone is that area of the bladder base bounded by the two ureteric orifices and the internal urethral orifice. Being relatively fixed at these points it is the least mobile part of the bladder and its appearance changes little with varying degrees of bladder distension. Its superficial muscle fibres are of relatively small diameter, giving it a smooth appearance on endoscopy compared with the often ridged or trabeculated appearance of the rest of the wall. Whilst the remainder of the bladder and urethra are formed from the urogenital sinus the trigone is formed by the incorporation of the lower end of the mesonephric ducts into the bladder base. Sensation in the lower urinary tract is difficult to quantify although it seems that sensation in the urethra is considerably more acute than elsewhere.

14.   **B E**
The pudendal nerve arises from the anterior surfaces of the S2, 3 and 4 nerve roots, whereas the nerve to obturator internus arises from the L5 and S1 and S2 roots. The pudendal nerve itself passes back between the pyriformis and coccygeus muscles to appear in the buttock between pyriformis and the sacrospinal ligament; thereafter it curves around the latter to run in the pudendal canal on the lateral wall of the ischio-rectal fossa. The inferior haemorrhoidal branch of the pudendal nerve supplies the subcutaneous and profundus portions of the external anal sphincter; the internal sphincter however receives autonomic supply from the pelvic plexus. Cutaneous branches of the pudendal nerve supply the clitoris (from the dorsal nerve of clitoris) the labia majora and minora (from the perineal branch) and the perianal skin (from the inferior haemorrhoidal branch).

15.   **A B D E**
The broad ligament is a double-layered fold of peritoneum lying on either side of the uterus; its medial edge is continuous with the serosa overlying the uterus and its lateral edge is attached to the pelvic side wall. The Fallopian tube lies in the medial three-quarters of its upper edge and the ovarian vessels in the lateral quarter of its upper edge. The ovary lies on the posterior surface of the broad ligament, its medial pole being attached to the cornu of the uterus by the ovarian ligament. The pelvic ureter passes forwards in the base of the broad ligament to enter obliquely into the base of the bladder. Apart from the structures already mentioned, the broad ligament contains a mass of areolar

tissue, the uterine blood vessels and lymphatics and vestigial remnants of the mesonephric (Wolffian) ducts, the epoophoron and the paroophoron.

16. **B D E**
The pelvic floor consists of a gutter-shaped sheet of striated muscle slung around the midline body effluents, the urethra, vagina and anal canal. Although functioning as a unit, it consists morphologically of three muscles, the ischiococcygeus ('coccygeus muscle'), the iliococcygeus and the pubococcygeus (together known as the levator ani), from behind forward, taking origin in turn from the ischial spine, the arcus tendineus and the posterior surface of the pubis. Anterior fibres of the pubococcygeus form a sling around the ano-rectal junction, joining with fibres from the opposite side and with posterior fibres of the profundus part of the external sphincter. Apart from the sphincteric functions of the muscles, they also help to maintain the position of the pelvic organs and to direct the internal rotation of the presenting part during labour. The nerve supply to the muscles is by the perineal branch of S4, the inferior haemorrhoidal and perineal nerves, from the sacral plexus.

17. **A B D E**
The ureter passes down the posterior abdominal wall on the psoas major muscle, being closely adherent to the overlying peritoneum. It passes over the genitofemoral nerve and enters the pelvis approximately at its midpoint, crossing the bifurcation of the common iliac artery. The ureter obtains its blood supply sequentially from branches of the renal arteries, the aorta, the gonadal arteries, the common and internal iliac arteries, and the superior and inferior vesical arteries. It may course very close to the infundibulo-pelvic ligament and this is one of the common sites of surgical injury to the ureter.

18. **A C D E**
Blood supply to the endometrium comes from the radial and spiral arteries. Subnuclear vacuolation of the glandular epithelium is an early sign of ovulation occurring within 36 hours after ovulation. Endometrial glands already developed by oestrogen influence become tortuous under the influence of progesterone in the second half of the cycle and accumulate secretions. Glandular secretion reduces in the latter part of the secretory phase if conception does not occur. The

walls of the coiled arteries constrict, closing off blood flow and producing ischaemia which leads to necrosis of the endometrium. The epithelial lining and the superficial portion of the lamina propria called the functional layer are sloughed during menstruation. The superficial compact and the deep spongy layers are noticeable before menstruation takes place.

19. **A B D**
The pituitary gland lies below and in front of the optic chiasma. The superior portion of the anterior part is known as the pars tuberalis. The anterior pituitary secretes six hormones: adrenocorticotrophic hormone, thyroid stimulating hormone, luteinising hormone, all under the stimulation of the hypothalamus and prolactin controlled by an inhibiting factor. Few nerve fibres pass between the anterior pituitary lobe and the hypothalamus but there is a direct link via the portal hypophyseal vessels and releasing factors can thereby be transferred. Vasopressin and oxytocin are released from the posterior pituitary gland.

20. **A C**
The endocervix has a secretory columnar epithelium which is maintained during menstruation. It is arranged in branched glands the secretion of which is scanty and viscid early in the follicular phase, becomes profuse and clear under the influence of oestrogen towards ovulation and then becomes thick, opaque and highly cellular with progesterone secretion in the luteal phase of the cycle. The corpus uteri has a largely muscular structure, the cervix a much larger fibrous content.

21. **B C D**
The mammary gland or breast lies in the superficial fascia. It is made up of 15-20 subunits of glandular tissue, whose lobules, enclosed in a fibro-areolar stroma, radiate from the nipple into the surrounding superficial fat. The periphery of the gland extends from the 2nd to the 6th rib in the vertical plane and from the side of the sternum to near the midaxillary line in the horizontal plane.

Two-thirds of the gland overlies the pectoralis major; one-third the serratus anterior. Although easily separated from the fascia covering these muscles, the gland is firmly connected to the true skin by suspensory ligaments of Cooper that pass from its stroma between lobules of fat.

In the pinkish areola surrounding the nipple there is a number of nodular rudimentary milk glands, the areolar glands and deep to the areola is some involuntary muscle, a lymph plexus and an absence of fat.

Innervation is via intercostal nerves (2nd to 6th) via lateral and anterior cutaneous branches. These or the vessels convey *sympathetic* fibres.

From a sub-areolar lymphatic plexus drainage occurs to pectoral and parasternal nodes. Axillary node dissection (sampling) forms an essential element of modern management of breast cancer.

22. **B C D E**
Gluteus minimus is supplied by the superior gluteal nerve.

The femoral nerve lies lateral to the femoral sheath and enters the thigh behind the inguinal ligament. It appears at the lateral border of psoas, runs downward in the angle between psoas and iliacus, but does not enter the femoral sheath, which encloses the femoral vessels. In the false pelvis, it supplies iliacus. Soon after crossing the inguinal ligament it breaks up into numerous motor and sensory branches. Two of these follow the artery, closely applied to its lateral side, into the adductor canal; one, the nerve to vastus medialis, is motor; the other, the saphenous nerve, is sensory. The femoral nerve supplies psoas and pectineus. The sartorius and rectus femoris are both supplied by one or two branches which enter them from 8 to 15 cm from the anterior superior spine.

23. **A B D E**
The great saphenous vein ascends throughout the length of the limb, in the subcutaneous fat. It begins at the medial end of the dorsal venous arch of the foot, passing in front of the medial malleolus, crossing the lower third of the medial surface of the tibia and following 1 cm behind its medial border as far as the knee. At the knee it is found on incising

a hand's breath behind the medial border of the patella. From there it takes a straight, but oblique, course up the thigh to the femoral vein which it joins 4 cm inferolateral to the pubic tubercle.

24. **A B C D**
The sciatic nerve arises from L4, L5, S1, 2, 3. From the lower border of the piriformis, it curves downward midway between the tuber ischii and the greater trochanter covered by gluteus maximus. The gluteal muscles are supplied by the gluteal nerves.

25. **A D**
The uterine artery arises from the internal iliac artery, descending in front of the ureter to the base of the broad ligament and at the lateral fornix of the vagina, it crosses above the ureter. After sending branches to the vagina and cervix, it continues tortuously up the side of the uterus between the layers of the broad ligament, supplying the uterus and the tubes, with free anastomosis. The round ligament is supplied from the external pudendal artery.

26. **A C D**
The labia minora develop from genital folds while labia majora develop from genital swellings. The lateral surface of the labia minora is keratinised.

27. **C D**
The Mullerian duct develops lateral to the Wolffian duct and is known as the paramesonephric duct. It develops on the lateral aspect of the mesonephros. It starts to disappear at 8-9 weeks due to the production of Mullerian inhibiting factor by the testis. It does not open into the sinus, but it protrudes against the posterior wall forming the Mullerian tubercles.

28. **B C E**
All diameters are absolutely greater in the female. The sacral promontory is more prominent in the male so that the male inlet is heart-shaped whereas the female inlet is more rounded, facilitating engagement of the fetal head. The female pubic arch is almost a right angle; it equals the angle between the outstretched thumb and the index finger. In the male it is an acute angle, equal to the angle between the index and middle fingers when spread. The acetabulum is

approximately its own diameter distant from the symphysis in the male, but in the female it is relatively much more.

29. A D E

The pelvic splanchnic nerves are also known as the nervi erigentes because they cause relaxation of the arteries to the erectile tissue, producing erection of the penis (or clitoris). They are parasympathetic nerves arising from S (2), 3, 4. They join the corresponding (sympathetic) hypogastric plexus which then becomes mixed sympathetic and parasympathetic.

30. A C

The coeliac trunk is the first of the three unpaired arteries that supply the gastro-intestinal tract. It arises from the aorta between the right and left crura of the diaphragm which straddle it. The pancreas lies below it. The coeliac trunk is only approximately 1 cm long. It is surrounded by the coeliac plexus of nerves. The coeliac trunk supplies the stomach, the adjacent parts of the oesophagus and duodenum and the three unpaired glands - liver, pancreas and spleen.

The branches are:
1. Left gastric
       oesophageal
       gastric
2. Splenic
       pancreatic
       splenic
       short gastric
       left gastro-epiploic
3. Hepatic
       gastro-duodenal
       right gastric
       right hepatic and cystic branch
       left hepatic

31. A B D E

The inguinal canal is an oblique tract through the anterior abdominal wall. It extends from the deep inguinal ring, a deficiency in the transversalis fascia just above the midpoint of the inguinal ligament to the superficial inguinal ring, a deficiency in the external oblique aponeurosis, lying just above the pubic tubercle. The anterior wall is formed by the external oblique aponeurosis and additionally laterally by the internal oblique. The posterior wall is formed by transversalis fascia throughout with the conjoint tendon medially. The canal is traversed by the spermatic cord in the male and the round ligament in the female.

32. B C D
The femoral sheath envelops the femoral artery, vein and some lymph vessels and is a prolongation of the extraperitoneal areolar tissue that envelops the external iliac vessels in the abdomen. The sheath is funnel-shaped, wider proximally and has three compartments.

BIOCHEMISTRY

The answers and teaching notes to this section start on page 22.

33. **The following statements concerning plasma lipids are correct:**

☐ A chylomicra are not normally present in the plasma of a person who has fasted 12 hours or more
☐ B in the fasting state circulating free fatty acids are absorbed to plasma albumin
☐ C high density lipoproteins contain most of the circulating cholesterol
☐ D the low density lipoprotein fraction corresponds to the beta lipoprotein fraction on electrophoresis
☐ E plasma free fatty acid concentration is reduced in the fasting state

34. **During the process of glucose production and metabolism**

☐ A the liver is the main organ of production
☐ B metabolism in the glycolytic pathway starts with glucose-6-phosphate
☐ C there is a net production of 4 molecules of ATP
☐ D the liver is the site of the gluco-regulatory action of glucogen
☐ E human growth hormone stimulates glucose uptake in fat and muscle

35. **A low level of potassium in the plasma may be caused by**

☐ A dehydration
☐ B thiazide diuretics
☐ C acidosis
☐ D primary hyperaldosteronism
☐ E a beta-cell tumour of the pancreas

36. **In sex steroid metabolism**

☐ A androstenedione is the main androgen
☐ B the normal ranges of testosterone in the male and female overlap
☐ C in women more than 50% of circulating testosterone is secreted by the adrenals
☐ D in women more than 50% of circulating dehydroepiandrosterone is ovarian in origin
☐ E testosterone and androstenedione are readily inter-convertible

TRALEE GENERAL HOSPITAL LIBRARY

33. A B D

Chylomicra are readily observed in lymph and plasma sampled three to four hours after a meal rich in fat. They are particles consisting mostly of triglycerides with some cholesterol, phospholipid and protein; they would not normally be present in the plasma of a person who has fasted twelve hours or more. In the fasting state free fatty acids are absorbed to plasma albumin. Cholesterol is predominantly contained in the low density lipoprotein fraction (beta fraction on electrophoresis). The high density fraction contains approximately 19% cholesterol compared to 47% for the low density.

34. A B D

The net gain is two molecules of ATP (the remaining two are used for phosphorylation). Human growth hormone inhibits glucose uptake.

35. B D E

Dehydration tends to increase rather than decrease the level of potassium in the plasma. Most of the potassium filtered by the kidney is reabsorbed in the proximal tubules and potassium is then secreted by the distal tubular cells. In the distal tubules sodium is generally reciprocally reabsorbed. In metabolic acidosis increased H^+ excretion by the kidney takes place, reducing potassium secretion and so plasma potassium is not decreased. Beta-cell tumours of the pancreas secrete insulin which promotes the intracellular passage of potassium reducing the plasma level. Thiazide diuretics act proximal to the distal tubule and increase sodium concentration in the distal tubular fluid and cause appreciable potassium loss in the urine. Individuals with primary hyperaldosteronism often become severely potassium depleted, probably by a similar mechanism.

36. A E

Average testosterone levels in the male are ten times higher than in the female and the normal ranges are quite separate. In the pre-menopausal woman 50% of circulating testosterone is derived from the conversion of ovarian (20%) and adrenal (30%) androstenedione, this being the main androgen produced by the ovaries and the interconversion readily achieved by the enzyme 17 beta hydroxysteroid dehydrogenase. Only 30% of circulating testosterone is actually secreted as such by the adrenal, but dehydro-epiandrosterone is produced almost exclusively by the adrenals.

BIOPHYSICS

The answers and teaching notes to this section start on page 24.

37. In medical imaging

- [ ] A computer assisted tomography (CT scanning) utilises high-power X-rays
- [ ] B diagnostic ultrasound utilises pulses of frequency 100 MHz
- [ ] C nuclear magnetic resonance imaging (NMR) involves the emission of low-frequency radiowaves
- [ ] D diagnostic X-ray work normally uses voltages between 50 and 150 kV
- [ ] E NMR may lead to ventricular fibrillation

38. Diagnostic X-rays

- [ ] A were discovered in 1885
- [ ] B utilise energies in the range 20-120 keV
- [ ] C are utilised in mammographic examination
- [ ] D production is based on acceleration of protons
- [ ] E utilise film containing silver halide

39. Radiotherapy

- [ ] A typically utilises 20 Gy given in fractions
- [ ] B target volume is the same as the tumour volume
- [ ] C usually utilises X-rays from linear accelerators operating in the range 4-25 MV for the treatment of deep-seated tumours
- [ ] D is not very effective in the treatment of cervical cancer
- [ ] E utilises low energy therapy (3-4 Mev) for treatment of vulvar carcinoma

40. The following are therapeutically radiosensitive tumours:

- [ ] A cervical carcinoma
- [ ] B vulvar carcinoma
- [ ] C carcinoma of breast
- [ ] D dysgerminoma
- [ ] E uterine sarcoma

37. A D E

CT scanning was developed in the 1970s to allow thin cross-sectional slices through the patient. The CT scan is a digital image produced by a computer from a large number of direct transmission measurements at different angles through the patient. It utilises a 120 kV X-ray tube and the computer reconstructs the image and displays it on a VDU, from which a hard copy may be taken using Polaroid film or by using a video converter to drive a multiformat image display camera.

Diagnostic ultrasound normally uses pulses of frequency 1 to 10 MHz from a special transducer. The time required for the sound pulses to travel to a reflecting surface within the body and back to a detector gives the depth of that surface.

NMR involves radiation from nuclei of radiowaves of very high frequency. These images represent primarily the proton concentration of tissues and techniques utilising different rates of decay of the magnetization signal means that tissues of similar proton concentration may be contrasted. NMR may in theory lead to ventricular fibrillation but there is a wide safety margin with clinical NMR.

38. B C E

Diagnostic X-rays were discovered by Roentgen in 1895 and were first used to treat gynaecological cancer in 1903. Mammography is based on the use of X-rays but X-rays tubes utilise a molybdenum target rather than tungsten. The generation of X-rays requires that electrons are accelerated through a potential difference so that they acquire sufficient energy to interact with the atoms of the target to produce X-rays.

39. C

Radiotherapy typically utilises 50 GY given in twenty fractions over 4 weeks, to minimise the risk of damage to adjacent normal tissues. The target volume is larger than the tumour volume to allow for microscopic spread of tumour cells. Radiotherapy is very effective in the treatment of cervical cancer. Low energy therapy may be useful in the treatment of skin conditions such as mycosis fungoides but is totally inadequate for the treatment of vulvar carcinoma.

40. **A B C D**

Cervical carcinoma is very radiosensitive, as is breast carcinoma. The management of dysgerminoma has been revolutionised by the use of radiotherapy and chemotherapy such that a condition with a previously very poor prognosis may now be cured. Vulvar carcinoma is radiosensitive but the adjacent normal skin is very sensitive making radiotherapy an option only for inoperable cases. Uterine sarcoma is not responsive to radiotherapy.

EMBRYOLOGY

The answers and teaching notes to this section start on page 29.

41. The following arise from Wolffian remnants:

- ☐ A the epoophoron
- ☐ B the processus vaginalis
- ☐ C the paroophoron
- ☐ D the round ligament
- ☐ E Gartner's duct

42. In the development of fetal sex organs

- ☐ A the presence of ovaries is necessary for the development of the paramesonephric ducts
- ☐ B the pronephric duct degenerates as the mesonephros develops
- ☐ C ova originate outside the developing gonad
- ☐ D the vagina is formed entirely by invagination of the paramesonephric ducts
- ☐ E sexual differentiation of the external genitalia is complete before the 10th week of life

43. In human fetal development

- ☐ A the primitive groove derives from the neural tube
- ☐ B the primitive streak lies caudal to the blastopore
- ☐ C the heart beat appears at 40 to 50 days post conception
- ☐ D at 6-8 weeks post conception the mid-gut protrudes through the umbilical cord
- ☐ E the decidua capsularis overlies the chorion frondosum

44. In fetal circulation

- ☐ A the foramen ovale permits blood to pass from the right to the left atrium
- ☐ B the ductus arteriosus carries blood from the pulmonary artery to the aorta
- ☐ C the ductus venosus carries blood to the inferior vena cava from the umbilical artery
- ☐ D the ductus arteriosus is contractile
- ☐ E the umbilical vein becomes the ligamentum teres of the adult

45. The following statements are correct:

☐ A the paramesonephric duct crosses the mesonephric duct ventrally to reach its medial side

☐ B the whole of the uterovaginal canal is formed by fusion of the two mesonephric ducts

☐ C the Mullerian tubercle is formed in the dorsal wall of the urogenital sinus

☐ D throughout fetal and early postnatal life the cervical portion of the uterus is larger than the body

☐ E the caudal part of the hindgut receives the allantois and is called the cloaca

46. Spermatogenesis

☐ A is a process requiring 110-120 days in the human male

☐ B requires both FSH and LH to stimulate sperm maturation

☐ C is associated with an increase in testosterone in the intertubular tissue of the testis

☐ D is abnormal in a male with karyotype 47XXY

☐ E would cease in the absence of testosterone

47. The Mullerian ducts

☐ A are derived from intermediate cell mass mesoderm

☐ B appear between the 8th and 9th weeks of embryonic development

☐ C develop lateral to the Wolffian ducts

☐ D fuse throughout their length by the 12th week of fetal development

☐ E become the sinovaginal bulbs in their lower part

48. Implantation

☐ A occurs two to three days following ovulation

☐ B in the human is described as interstitial

☐ C is associated with decidualisation of the endometrium

☐ D is complete by about 10 days

☐ E normally occurs in the lower portion of the uterus

41. A C E

Occasionally almost the whole of the mesonephric duct persists and is then known as Gartner's duct. The epoophoron and paroophoron arise from Wolffian remnants. The processus vaginalis is a diverticulum from the coelomic cavity; it becomes a herniation of peritoneum into the scrotum to receive the descending testis. The round ligament is of mesodermal origin.

42. C

The pronephros represents a primitive form of kidney in certain mammals. In man this form of excretory apparatus is rudimentary, but acts as an organiser for the mesonephric ducts. Normal development of paramesonephric ducts may occur in the presence of streak gonads. The ova originate in the yolk sac wall and migrate via the innermost layer of the dorsal body wall and thence into the developing genital ridge. At least part (possibly all) of the vagina is formed from the urogenital sinus. Sexual differentiation is not complete before the tenth week of life.

43. B D

The primitive groove is formed from the primitive streak due to lateral accumulation of mesoderm. The fetal heart beat appears at 21 to 28 days post conception. After 8 weeks the mid-gut is withdrawn from the umbilical cord. The decidua capsularis overlies the chorion laeve.

44. A B D E

The ductus venosus runs from the left side of the portal sinus to the hepato-cardiac channel, thus short-circuiting the hepatic sinusoids.

45. A C D E

Caudally the paramesonephric duct crosses the mesonephric duct to reach its medial side where it meets the duct of the other side in the urogenital septum. The two paramesonephric ducts eventually completely fuse in their lower part and the septum breaks down to form the utero-vaginal canal. The caudal tip of the uterovaginal canal comes into contact with the dorsal wall of the urogenital sinus where it produces an elevation, the Mullerian tubercle. Throughout fetal and early postnatal life the cervical portion of the uterus is larger than the body and only alters in later life under hormonal influence. The caudal portion of the hind gut which receives the allantois is slightly dilated and called the cloaca; it is separated from the exterior by the cloacal membrane.

46. **B C D E**
Spermatogenesis, the formation of a mature sperm from a primitive germ cell takes approximately 70 days in the human male. FSH acts directly upon Sertoli cells to facilitate spermatogenesis; a second requirement is for testosterone which is produced by the Leydig cells of the testis in the intertubular tissue under the influence of LH and then transferred into the tubular lumen. The 47XXY chromosomal pattern produces the syndrome of Klinefelter or seminiferous tubule dysgenesis. The external genitalia are normal male, as testosterone production is often sufficient for male secondary sexual characteristics to develop although the testes are usually small.

47. **C**
The Mullerian or paramesonephric ducts develop lateral to the Wolffian or mesonephric ducts as an invagination of the coelomic epithelium overlying the nephrogenic ridge, at 5-6 weeks embryonic development. The lower end of each Mullerian duct fuses with a thickening on the posterior aspect of the urogenital sinus known as the sinovaginal bulb. Their junctions form the vaginal plate, a solid core of epithelium which becomes canalised at 16-18 weeks. The Mullerian ducts themselves fuse in their lower part to form the uterovaginal primordium by 12 weeks, although the cranial portions of the ducts remain separate and ultimately give rise to the Fallopian tubes.

48. **B C D**
On the fourth to fifth day after ovulation the ovum enters the uterine cavity in the form of a morula or perhaps an early blastocyst. One or two days later the process of implantation begins with swelling of the blastocyst and disappearance of the zona pellucida. Amniotic epithelium is formed from the inner layer of the polar trophoblast and becomes separated from the embryonic cell mass by the appearance of an amniotic cavity. The polar trophoblast becomes attached to the uterine epithelium and begins to burrow into the endometrium. The surface cells of the penetrating trophoblast fuse to form a layer of syncitiotrophoblast arising from the cellular cytotrophoblast on its embryonic aspect. Endometrial invasion is complete after about 10 days and occurs usually high on the posterior wall.

ENDOCRINOLOGY

The answers and teaching notes to this section start on page 36.

49. In the normal adult adrenal gland

- [ ] A aldosterone is produced in the zona glomerulosa
- [ ] B the cortex has a diurnal rhythm
- [ ] C aldosterone production is purely under control of ACTH
- [ ] D the zona glomerulosa forms the greater part of the cortex
- [ ] E cortisol production is under ACTH control

50. Prolactin

- [ ] A is produced by the anterior pituitary
- [ ] B concentration in the plasma rises in human pregnancy
- [ ] C production is increased by thyroid stimulating hormone-releasing hormone
- [ ] D plasma concentrations fall by 50% or more just before delivery in the human
- [ ] E has a long half-life in the circulation

51. The following statements are correct

- [ ] A thyroid stimulating hormone (TSH) is a polypeptide
- [ ] B thyroxine and tri-iodothyronine are the same
- [ ] C thyroxine stimulates oxygen consumption
- [ ] D congenital hypothyroidism (cretinism) may result from untreated maternal thyrotoxicosis (hyperthyroidism)
- [ ] E the inactive thyroid gland shows an increased amount of colloid

52. Insulin

- [ ] A is a glycoprotein
- [ ] B is produced by the alpha cells
- [ ] C levels decrease and glucagon levels increase in response to hypoglycaemia
- [ ] D is not required by exercising muscle to utilise glucose
- [ ] E facilitates glycogen breakdown and increases glucose output from the liver

53. Human chorionic gonadotrophin (HCG)

☐ A reaches a maximum at the end of pregnancy
☐ B serves as a tumour marker
☐ C production begins before the corpus luteum of pregnancy
☐ D is increased in hydatidiform mole
☐ E is the basis of most laboratory pregnancy tests

54. Oxytocin

☐ A is synthesised by the pituitary gland
☐ B rises in concentration in maternal blood before the onset of labour
☐ C causes milk ejection
☐ D is acted upon by oxytocinase
☐ E has biological properties overlapping with vasopressin

55. Glucocorticoids

☐ A have their major effect on intermediary metabolism i.e. protein-carbohydrate interconversion
☐ B cause an increase in total body water content
☐ C are needed to increase liver storage of glycogen
☐ D have a negative feedback effect on ACTH (corticotrophin)
☐ E are C17 steroids

56. Progesterone is

☐ A synthesised by the trophoblast
☐ B mainly excreted as pregnanediol glucuronide
☐ C synthesised from cholesterol
☐ D a smooth muscle stimulant
☐ E a glycoprotein

57. Progestogens

☐ A reduce cervical mucus ferning
☐ B cause cessation of endometrial gland proliferation
☐ C increase the permeability of cervical mucus to sperms
☐ D are responsible for the hypertensive change in women taking combined oral contraceptives
☐ E inhibit uterine muscle activity

58. Human chorionic gonadotrophin (HCG)

☐ A is produced by the trophoblast
☐ B is produced by fetal liver
☐ C may be immunosuppressive
☐ D reaches a peak in the second trimester of pregnancy
☐ E is produced by some non-trophoblastic tumours

59. The following statements concerning maternal and fetal thyroid function are correct:

☐ A the fetal thyroid traps iodine from the 6th week of gestation onwards
☐ B the fetal pituitary starts to secrete TSH in the second trimester
☐ C maternal TSH freely crosses the placental barrier
☐ D cretins have high TSH levels in the first week of life
☐ E levels of free thyroxine are lower in pregnancy than in a non-pregnant adult

60. Human placental lactogen (HPL)

☐ A increases insulin resistance
☐ B promotes fat mobilisation
☐ C cannot be detected in maternal serum until the 14th week of pregnancy
☐ D shows an elevated level in twin pregnancy
☐ E shows a normal level in trophoblastic disease

61. Cyproterone acetate

☐ A decreases gonadotrophin secretion
☐ B is used to induce ovulation
☐ C is used in the treatment of virilism
☐ D is safe in pregnant patients
☐ E exhibits strong progestogenic activity when acetylated

62. Raised serum levels of follicle stimulating hormone (FSH) are found in

☐ A association with combined oestrogen/progesterone contraceptive use
☐ B post-menopausal women
☐ C Sheehan's syndrome
☐ D Turner's syndrome
☐ E pure gonadal dysgenesis

63. Cortisol

☐ A is produced by the zona glomerulosa of the adrenal cortex
☐ B has a diurnal rhythm with its lowest level present in the morning
☐ C is excreted in the urine as a 17 oxogenic steroid
☐ D production is increased by hypoglycaemia
☐ E when produced in excess is associated with generalised obesity

64. The pituitary gland

☐ A arises from mesoderm
☐ B lies posterior to the cerebellum
☐ C lies below the hypothalamus
☐ D has basophil cells which secrete LH
☐ E has acidophil cells which secrete ACTH

65. Aldosterone

- ☐ A is secreted by cells of the zona glomerulosa
- ☐ B production is increased by a fall in plasma renin
- ☐ C production is increased by a decrease in plasma osmolality
- ☐ D levels rise in normal pregnancy
- ☐ E is secreted in response to hyperkalaemia

66. Oxytocin

- ☐ A has an antidiuretic effect
- ☐ B is produced by the anterior pituitary
- ☐ C stimulates milk formation
- ☐ D is a steroid hormone
- ☐ E has effects on the uterus which are potentiated by oestrogen

67. Oestrogen receptors

- ☐ A are polypeptide hormones
- ☐ B are present in all oestrogen target tissues
- ☐ C are present in breast cancers
- ☐ D bind clomiphene
- ☐ E can be measured to predict response of endometrial cancer to hormone therapy

68. In normal pregnancy

- ☐ A there are equal increases in the excretion of oestrone, oestradiol and oestriol
- ☐ B serum HCG concentration rises to a peak at 20 weeks' gestation
- ☐ C there is a reduced aldosterone secretion
- ☐ D androgen excretion is reduced
- ☐ E there is an increase in serum protein-bound iodine

49. A B E

Aldosterone is synthesised principally by the cells of the zona glomerulosa. Cortisol is produced in the zona reticularis and is under control of ACTH, secreted by the basophil cells of the pars anterior of the pituitary gland. Aldosterone is not under direct ACTH control, but release is mediated through sodium levels via the renin-angiotensin system. The circadian rhythm is maintained by pituitary ACTH secretion and mediated by variation in corticotrophin-releasing factor secretion from the median eminence of the hypothalamus. The zona fasiculata forms the greater part of the cortex and is probably a non-secretory zone of 'reserve' cells.

50. A B C

Prolactin is produced by the anterior pituitary, kept under tonic inhibition by secretion of a prolactin inhibiting hormone. Prolactin is secreted in the middle trimester of pregnancy and increases progressively towards term. There is no fall just before delivery. On the contrary, levels rise further and are maintained as long as breast feeding continues. Prolactin has a very short half-life in the circulation. TRH may lead to both TSH and prolactin release.

51. C E

Thyroid-stimulating hormone is a glycoprotein. Thyroxine is tetra-iodothyronine. The major action of thyroid hormones is to stimulate oxygen consumption. Cretinism may result from overtreatment of the mother with antithyroid drugs or severe maternal hypothyroidism. T3 and T4 are stored in the colloid vesicles of the follicles of the thyroid gland bound to thyroglobulin. Their release is stimulated by TSH. The inactive gland therefore shows an increased amount of colloid.

52. C D

Insulin is a polypeptide with two amino acid chains. It is produced by the beta cells of the islets of Langerhans; the alpha cells produce glucagon. Glucagon has a hyperglycaemic effect and levels increase in response to hypoglycaemia. In the normal subject, insulin has a hypoglycaemic effect. Insulin is not required by exercising muscle to utilise glucose; it decreases glucose output from the liver and facilitates glycogen synthesis.

53. B C D E

Implantation is probably well underway by 5-6 days post-ovulation and HCG produced by the blastocyst to convert the corpus luteum in early pregnancy can be detected in maternal serum using a sensitive beta-HCG assay by 8 days post-ovulation. HCG rises rapidly in early pregnancy reaching a peak between 56 and 68 days after ovulation. Thereafter levels fall to 18 weeks after which they remain more or less constant until after delivery. HCG serves as the basis for most pregnancy tests. Pathologically high concentrations of HCG are seen in hydatidiform mole. Radioimmunoassay of HCG in urine is used in the follow up of hydatidiform molar pregnancy and also to judge the efficacy of chemotherapy in chorioncarcinoma where it serves as an excellent tumour marker.

54. C D E

The posterior pituitary gland secretes two hormones, oxytocin and arginine vasopressin. Both hormones are synthesised in the cell bodies of neurones in the supraoptic and paraventricular nuclei and transferred down their axons to the posterior pituitary. The principal physiological effect of oxytocin is on the myoepithelial cells of the breast ducts promoting milk ejection. Oxytocin also causes uterine smooth muscle contraction but it increases only once labour is established. Oxytocin is inactivated by oxytocinase produced by the placenta. Oxytocin has biological properties which overlap to some extent with vasopressin, in particular an antidiuretic effect.

55. A C D

The adrenal cortex secretes glucocorticoids, C21 steroids with widespread effects on the metabolism of carbohydrate and protein. The C21 steroids have both mineralocorticoid and glucocorticoid activity; mineralocorticoids are those with predominant effects on sodium and potassium excretion and glucocorticoids are those which particularly affect glucose and protein metabolism. The two common glucocorticoids are cortisol and corticosterone, their actions including increased protein catabolism and hepatic glycogenesis and gluconeogenesis. Glucose-6-phosphate activity is increased and the blood glucose rises. Glucocorticoids inhibit ACTH secretion and ACTH secretion is increased in adrenalectomised animals. Adrenal insufficiency is characterised by an inability to excrete a water load and only glucocorticoids repair this deficit; the exact mechanism of glucocorticoid water excretion is contentious.

56. **A B C**

Progesterone is a steroid hormone produced in the luteinised granulosa cells of the ovarian corpus luteum. During early pregnancy, between 5-7 weeks following the LMP placental trophoblast takes over progesterone production utilising cholesterol as the major precursor. It has a short half-life and is converted in the liver to pregnanediol, which is conjugated to glucuronic acid and excreted in the urine. Progesterone facilitates the secretory changes in the endometrium necessary for implantation of the fertilised ovum and it acts also as a smooth muscle relaxant hence suppressing uterine contractility.

57. **A B E**

Substances which mimic the action of progesterone may be called progestogens. Progesterone prepares the endometrium for implantation and maintenance of pregnancy. Therefore it causes secretory changes in the endometrium, gland promotion rather than regression and it suppresses uterine excitability. It is progesterone which causes the loss of cervical mucus ferning after ovulation. Oestrogens rather than progestogens are thought to be responsible for the hypertensive implications of oral contraceptives. Progestogens reduce the permeability of cervical mucus to sperms.

58. **A C E**

Human chorionic gonadotrophin (HCG) is produced by the placental trophoblast and some other tissues but not by fetal liver. The level in maternal serum rises rapidly in early pregnancy reaching a peak between 8 and 10 weeks of pregnancy. There is then a rapid reduction to 18 weeks after which levels remain more or less constant until delivery. HCG almost certainly rescues the corpus luteum from dissolution and promotes placental steroidogenesis. It is also important in the induction of fetal testosterone secretion by Leydig cells in the male fetus. It is suggested that HCG mediates the immunological privilege afforded to the fetus. A variety of gonadal and non-gonadal tumours have been reported to produce HCG; these include tumours of lung, stomach, liver, breast, kidney, pancreas, ovary and testis, carcinoid tumours and lymphomas.

59. **B D**

During pregnancy, thyroid hormone binding globulin levels increase in the first trimester under the influence of oestrogen; T3 and T4 production are increased but the free levels of these hormones are unchanged. Neither TSH nor thyroid hormones themselves cross the placenta to any significant extent.

The developing thyroid is first recognised as a thickening on the floor of the pharynx at around 4 weeks gestation; it does not begin to function however until the end of the first trimester. Fetal TSH production begins at around the same time and levels increase steadily between 20 and 30 weeks gestation, increasing further after delivery, but usually returning to normal adult levels within 3 days. In cretinism the deficiency of thyroid hormone leads to a persistently elevated TSH level.

60. **A B D**

Human placental lactogen is not detectable in the non-pregnant female but can be detected from 5 weeks' gestation, its concentration increasing with advanced gestation to around 35 weeks. The shape of the concentration curve closely resembles that of placental growth and levels tend to be increased in situations associated with increased placental weight e.g. multiple pregnancy. It has both growth hormone and prolactin like properties and among its metabolic effects are an increase in plasma free fatty acids due to maternal fat mobilisation and an increased insulin resistance causing higher circulating insulin and an increased insulin response to a glucose load.

61. **A C E**

Cyproterone acetate is a 17-alpha-methyl-beta-testosterone which acts as an anti-androgen at the hair follicle level, competing with testosterone for receptors; it also decreases gonadotrophin production centrally. It is used in the treatment of hirsutism and virilism usually combined with an oestrogen preparation. It tends to suppress ovulation. The safety of cyproterone in pregnancy has not been demonstrated; it is known to cause feminisation of the fetus in rats.

62. **B D E**

Follicle stimulating hormone (FSH) is secreted by the basophil cells of the anterior pituitary, release being governed by gonadal steroids acting at a hypothalamic level modulating the production of gonadotrophin releasing hormone and also directly on the pituitary. Oestrogen has both negative and positive feedback effects and alters the proportion of LH and FSH secreted in response to GnRH. Low oestrogen status e.g. in the post-menopausal woman, in Turner's syndrome and in pure gonadal dysgenesis are all characterised by grossly elevated FSH levels. In Sheehan's syndrome, pan-hypopituitarism results from post partum hypoxic pituitary necrosis. FSH levels are inevitably low. Combined oestrogen-progesterone contraceptive pills inhibit ovulation by interference with feedback mechanisms at the hypothalamic level.

63. C D

Cortisol is produced from the zona fasiculata of the adrenal cortex; the zona glomerulosa secretes aldosterone. There is a diurnal rhythm of ACTH secretion initiated by the hypothalamus which leads to variation in cortisol output, levels being maximal between 6 and 8 am and lowest at midnight. Production of cortisol is increased in response to hypoglycaemia. This results in an increase in gluconeogenesis, peripheral antagonism to insulin and normo- or hyperglycaemia.

The substances assayed in the urine as 17 oxogenic steroids are essentially derived from the 17 hydroxycorticosteroids cortisol, cortisone and their tetrahydro derivatives. The obesity of Cushing's syndrome is typically truncal, being maximal on the face, supraclavicular fossae and over the 7th cervical vertebra, the limbs being relatively spared.

64. C D

The pituitary gland arises from the ectoderm of Rathke's pouch and lies anterior to the cerebellum. It lies below the hypothalamus, from which various releasing factors pass to the pituitary. Basophil cells secrete LH and also TSH, FSH and ACTH.

65. A D

Aldosterone is produced by the cells of the zona glomerulosa of the adrenal cortex. It is secreted in response to increased levels of circulating angiotensin II. Renin is secreted by the juxtaglomerular cells of the kidney in response to decreased renal perfusion, decreased ECF volume or sodium depletion; it acts on the alpha-2 globulin

GENETICS

The answers and teaching notes to this section start on page 46.

69. In human genetics

- [ ] A the total number of chromosomes in both normal males and females is 46
- [ ] B in the female, the sex chromosomes are XY
- [ ] C chromatin positive cells (Barr body present) are characteristic of normal males
- [ ] D the sexual differentiation of the fetal gonads occurs about the 7th week
- [ ] E the Y chromosome determines the development of the ovary

70. The following statements about haemophilia are true:

- [ ] A all sons of affected males will inherit the condition
- [ ] B half sons of a carrier female will inherit the condition
- [ ] C normal daughters cannot be born to a carrier female
- [ ] D the incidence of haemophilia in the daughters of an affected male (married to a normal female) will be one in four
- [ ] E if a carrier female marries an affected male, all of the offspring will inherit the haemophilia gene

71. The following conditions are X-linked:

- [ ] A congenital adrenal hyperplasia
- [ ] B Duchenne muscular dystrophy
- [ ] C classical achondroplasia
- [ ] D true hermaphroditism
- [ ] E Hurler's syndrome

72. In Down's syndrome

- [ ] A most patients have an extra number 21 chromosome
- [ ] B trisomy is usually due to non-disjunction during meiosis
- [ ] C a female with Down's syndrome would never have a normal child
- [ ] D women over the age of 40 years have a risk of 1 in 200 of having a child with Down's syndrome
- [ ] E an affected fetus may be associated with a reduced alpha-fetoprotein concentration in amniotic fluid

73. **There is a recognisable chromosome abnormality in the following:**

- [ ] A Klinefelter's syndrome
- [ ] B Tay-Sach's disease
- [ ] C achondroplasia
- [ ] D Cri du chat syndrome
- [ ] E Patau's syndrome

74. **Chromosomes**

- [ ] A are usually studied after 12-24 hours culture of peripheral blood
- [ ] B are most easily identified during interphase
- [ ] C are reduced in number during the first stage of meiosis
- [ ] D are arrested in their division at anaphase to facilitate analysis in the laboratory
- [ ] E normally number 45

75. **Alleles are**

- [ ] A structural gene products
- [ ] B regulatory gene products
- [ ] C dominant genes
- [ ] D non-identical genes at the same locus
- [ ] E broken off gene fragments

76. **In meiosis**

- [ ] A chiasmata form during the zygotene phase
- [ ] B chromatids form during the pachytene phase
- [ ] C primary arrest of meiosis in the oocyte takes place in the diplotene phase
- [ ] D each stage occurs twice
- [ ] E reduction of chromosome number takes place in the first division

77. In the cell cycle

- [ ] A DNA is synthesised during the S(synthesis) phase
- [ ] B G2(resting phase) precedes mitosis
- [ ] C mitosis normally takes longer than S phase
- [ ] D phase durations may be calculated from 'percentage of labelled mitosis' curves
- [ ] E the shortest phase of mitosis is anaphase

78. Testicular feminisation is characterised by

- [ ] A XY mosaicism
- [ ] B a hypoplastic uterus
- [ ] C chromatin positivity
- [ ] D poorly developed breasts
- [ ] E pure gonadal dysgenesis

79. Mongolism

- [ ] A affects 1 in 2000 of all conceptions
- [ ] B results from trisomy 21
- [ ] C is the commonest sex-linked abnormality
- [ ] D incidence increases with increasing maternal age
- [ ] E may be detected by exfoliated fetal cells

80. In Turner's syndrome

- [ ] A the patient usually has primary amenorrhoea
- [ ] B the karyotype is 45XO
- [ ] C the patient is usually tall
- [ ] D there is poor breast development
- [ ] E mental retardation is common

69. A D

In the female, the sex chromosomes are normally XX. Barr observed that a large proportion of interphase nuclei from female tissues contained a characteristic small condensed mass of chromatin often lying against the nuclear membrane. It is believed that all female cells contain the sex chromatin (Barr body). The Y chromosome determines testicular development. Up to the seventh week of development the appearance of the external genitalia is similar in both sexes.

70. B

Haemophilia is inherited as a sex-linked recessive condition. Therefore sons of an affected male are unaffected, as they inherit the Y chromosome. Half of the sons of a carrier female will inherit the condition (one of the X chromosomes in the carrier female carries the gene). Similarly half the daughters of a female carrier will inherit a normal X chromosome from both parents. Because the gene is recessive, all daughters born to an affected male and normal female will be carriers. To exhibit the disease both X chromosomes would require to carry the gene (as would occur if parents were a haemophiliac male and a carrier female). However, an affected male and carrier female have a 50% chance of producing a normal male offspring.

71. B D

Congenital adrenal hyperplasia is an autosomal recessive disorder which is more often recognised in females, but is not truly X-linked as it is also seen in males. Classical achondroplasia is an autosomal dominant disorder. Hurler's syndrome is a severe autosomal recessive mucopolysaccharidosis (Hunter's syndrome is the X-linked disease). Duchenne muscular dystrophy and true hermaphroditism are both X-linked conditions.

72. A B E

Down's syndrome involves an excess of chromosome 21 material but in 4% of cases this does not amount to a separate chromosome. It most frequently arises due to non-separation of the chromosomes during meiosis. A female with Down's syndrome has a 1 in 2 chance of having a normal child. After the age of 40 the risk of an affected child is more than 1 in 100. Although the diagnosis of Down's syndrome should rest upon cytological culture from amniotic fluid and genetic studies, it is associated with reduced amniotic fluid alpha-fetoprotein.

73. **A D E**

Klinefelter's syndrome characteristically has an XXY chromosome complement. Cri du chat syndrome is apparently due to deletion of part of the short arm of chromosome 5. Patau's syndrome displays trisomy 13. Tay-Sach's disease is associated with a single autosomal recessive gene and achondroplasia is due to an autosomal dominant gene neither of which is normally recognisable without special techniques.

74. **C**

Chromosome studies of peripheral white blood cells usually require at least 72 hours of incubation. Colchicine is added to the medium to arrest mitosis at metaphase, by disrupting the mitotic spindle. It is in metaphase that chromosomes are most readily identified. Meiosis is a mechanism for reducing chromosome numbers, each daughter cell receiving half (23) the normal complement of 46 chromosomes.

75. **D**

Alleles are alternative forms of a gene that may occupy the same locus; any one chromosome bears only a single allele at any given locus, although in the population as a whole there may be multiple alleles, dominant or recessive, any one of which may occupy that locus. They are thus complete genes, not parts of a gene or products of a gene.

76. **B C E**

Cross-over starts in diplotene. Zygotene is the stage of pairing of homologous chromosomes. There are more cross-overs in the oocyte than in the spermatocyte. Chromatids result from the condensation of duplicated chromatin. Meiosis resumes 36 hours before ovulation. There is no prophase in the second division, which involves separation but not duplication.

77. **A D E**

DNA is synthesised during the S-phase which follows a resting phase (G1) which occurs after mitosis. A further resting phase (G2) follows the S- phase. Some cells become non-dividing and leave the cycle whilst others enter a more prolonged resting (G0) phase. The S-phase takes substantially longer than mitosis, whose phase durations may be estimated by the standard 'percentage of labelled mitoses' technique. The phases of mitosis are prophase, metaphase, anaphase and telophase. The latter is the longest phase, with anaphase being the shortest.

78. **All False**
The genotype XY is associated with testicular feminisation or pure gonadal dysgenesis, but mosaics are not usually found. Having one X chromosome, patients are chromatin negative. Patients with testicular feminisation have a blind vagina, no uterus, but well-developed breasts. Gonadal dysgenesis is associated with streak gonads and a hypoplastic uterus.

79. **B D E**
Mongolism is trisomy 21 and affects 1 in 650 of all conceptions, with the incidence increasing with increasing maternal age. It is an autosomal, not a sex chromosome abnormality and may be detected in culture of exfoliated fetal cells in amniotic fluid.

80. **A B D**
Turner's syndrome is characterised by the karyotype 45XO. Primary amenorrhoea is common and breast development is poor. Mental retardation is not normally a feature.

IMMUNOLOGY AND HAEMATOLOGY

The answers and teaching notes to this section start on page 52.

81. The following statements concerning immunoglobulins are correct:

- [ ] A they are all gamma-globulins
- [ ] B the five classes of immunoglobulins differ in their heavy polypeptide chains
- [ ] C IgG crosses the placental barrier
- [ ] D IgM is produced as the primary response to an antigen
- [ ] E IgE is predominantly found in the plasma

82. Lymphokines

- [ ] A are all antibodies arising from mast cells
- [ ] B arise from plasma cells
- [ ] C are IgE immunoglobulins
- [ ] D are responsible for immune complex formation
- [ ] E are produced by Type IV cell-mediated immune responses

83. Passive immunisation is used in the prophylaxis of the following conditions:

- [ ] A actinomycosis
- [ ] B pertussis
- [ ] C rubella in pregnancy
- [ ] D syphilis
- [ ] E tuberculosis

84. The T-lymphocyte population

- [ ] A is responsible for cell-mediated immune response
- [ ] B recirculates through the reticulo-endothelial system
- [ ] C populates the paracortical areas of the central lymphoid tissue
- [ ] D comprises 70% of blood lymphocytes
- [ ] E arises from stem cells in the thymus

85. **The following statements concerning haemostasis are correct**

☐ A tissue thromboplastin activates factor VII
☐ B plasmin converts fibrin polymers to insoluble fibrin
☐ C in small blood vessels platelet aggregation follows fibrin deposition
☐ D thrombasthenia is the term used to describe platelet deficiency
☐ E prothrombin is vitamin-K dependent

86. **The following statements relating to the haemopoietic tissues are correct:**

☐ A red marrow is present in the bones of the vault of the adult skull
☐ B sinusoids in marrow are lined by typical endothelial cells
☐ C lymphocytes are produced in bone marrow
☐ D the red cell nucleus is extruded at the polychromatophilic erythroblast stage
☐ E megakaryocytes are polyploid

87. **The following are essential for erythrocyte production:**

☐ A iron
☐ B folic acid
☐ C nicotinic acid
☐ D vitamin B12
☐ E myoglobin

88. **Lymph**

☐ A contains no cells
☐ B contains lipase
☐ C has a protein content higher than that of plasma
☐ D capillaries are found in the superficial layer of the skin
☐ E channels contain smooth muscle

89. White blood cells

- ☐ A are present in blood in concentrations of 4,000 to 10,000 per litre
- ☐ B are synthesised mainly in lymphoid tissue
- ☐ C have a circulation time of 90 days
- ☐ D include monocytes which comprise 10-15% of the total
- ☐ E produce heparin

90. Red blood cells (erythrocytes)

- ☐ A have a lifespan of 120 days
- ☐ B are nucleated
- ☐ C require vitamin D for synthesis
- ☐ D production is stimulated by erythropoietin
- ☐ E are produced partially in the spleen of adults

91. Lymph

- ☐ A contains no cells
- ☐ B may clot
- ☐ C capillaries are found in the superficial layer of the skin
- ☐ D protein content draining the legs is 40% that of plasma
- ☐ E contains lipase

92. Macrophages

- ☐ A produce antibody in response to antigenic stimulation
- ☐ B are motile
- ☐ C are phagocytic
- ☐ D have lysosomes in their cytoplasm
- ☐ E are derived from polymorphonuclear leucocytes

81. **B C D**

The majority of immunoglobulins are gamma-globulins but there is some electrophoretic activity in the alpha and beta regions. The classes resemble each other in that the molecules are composed of two identical light polypeptide chains and two identical heavy chains. The difference lies in their heavy chains. However, in any one class there are two types, differing in the light chains. IgG is of sufficiently low molecular weight to cross the placenta. The first-formed antibodies are of IgM type; IgG appears later. IgE is present in extremely small amounts in plasma; it is the tissue antibody responsible for atopic hypersensitivity.

82. **E**

In type IV cell-mediated immunity, sensitised lymphocytes come into contact with an appropriate antigen and release a number of effector proteins, called lymphokines. These include migration inhibition factor, lymphotoxin, chemotactic factor and interferon. They do not arise from mast cells or plasma cells, nor are they thought to be responsible for immune complex formation but information on the subject of lymphokines is scanty at present.

83. **C**

Transient immunity to some infections can be achieved by passive transfer of appropriate antibodies by injection of serum from an immune individual or animal. Rubella is the only one of the above listed diseases in which passive immunity is employed. It is effective only if given before exposure and efficacy is doubtful. Specific antibodies cannot be raised against the antigens of the others.

84. **A B C D**

Lymphoid stem cells may first be detected in the yolk sac, later in the fetal liver and subsequently in the bone marrow. They subsequently may mature within the bone marrow (B cells) or migrate to the thymus (T cells) where they populate the area around the periphery of the thymic cortex. T cells are responsible for cell mediated immunity whereas the B cells are responsible for humoral or antibody mediated immunity. T lymphocytes comprise around 70% of the 'recirculating pool' of lymphocytes in peripheral blood and lymph nodes whereas B lymphocytes predominate in the marrow and spleen.

85. A E

The first step in the extrinsic pathway is the formation of a complex between tissue factors and factor VII. Plasmin acts on fibrinogen and fibrin, splitting them into a heterogenous mixture of small peptides known collectively as fibrin degradation products. Platelet aggregation is the primary event in coagulation in small blood vessels. Thrombasthenia is an autosomal recessive disorder resulting in a haemorrhagic tendency, the platelets failing to aggregate properly. Platelet deficiency is thrombocytopenia. Vitamin K is essential for the 8-carboxylation of specific glutamic acid residues in factors II, VII, IX and X; without it these factors do not bind calcium and do not form complexes with phospholipid.

86. A B C E

Red marrow is present in the bones of the vault of the adult skull. The red cell nucleus is extruded at the normoblastic stage. Lymphocytes are normally formed in the lymphoid tissue of the bone marrow, thymus, spleen and lymph nodes. Normal megakaryocytes are polyploid. Megakaryocyte abnormalities may include small mononuclear or binuclear forms.

87. A B D

Normal erythropoiesis is dependent on adequate supplies of:

Amino acids – for the synthesis of the globin component of haemoglobin and the red cell stroma

Iron – which is essential for the formation of haem prosthetic groups

Vitamin B12 – is necessary in nucleic acid synthesis in particular for the synthesis of labile methyl groups from one carbon precursor

Folic acid – is also necessary in nucleic acid synthesis for the movement of methyl groups from one acceptor to another

Vitamin B6 – appears to function as a co-enzyme in the formation of haem.

88. **A B E**

The lymphatic system drains the excess tissue fluid, transports absorbed substances (especially fats) away from the gastrointestinal tract and acts as a system for the circulation of lymphocytes. It has a high protein content, but in the legs, for example, the protein content is only 10% of that in plasma. Lymph contains clotting factors and enzymes such as lipase and histaminase. The lymphatics arise as blind-ended capillaries in all tissues except the superficial layers of the skin, the central nervous system and bone. Lymph channels contain smooth muscle which contracts, assisting movement along the channels.

89. **A E**

The three types of white cells are granulocytes (50-75%), lymphocytes (20-40%) and monocytes, which comprise only 2 to 8% of leucocytes. Circulation time is very short, with granulocytes, for example, spending an average of only two days in the circulation. Most white cells are produced in the bone marrow, although lymphocytes are produced in lymphoid tissues. Basophil granulocytes produce histamine and heparin. White cells are attracted by for example bacterial toxins and have the capacity to engulf and phagocytose material.

90. **A D**

Red cells are chiefly responsible for the transport of oxygen. They have a life-span of 120 days, but do not have nuclei and therefore cannot synthesise protein. They contain also carbonic anhydrase, which helps in the transport of carbon dioxide. Vitamin B12 and folic acid are necessary for red cell synthesis, but vitamin D is not essential for this function. Red cells are manufactured in the fetus in the spleen, but during the latter part of gestation and after birth it is limited to the bone marrow. Erythropoietin is a glycoprotein produced by the kidney and released in response to need such as haemorrhage.

91. **E**

See answer to question 88.

92. **B C D**

Macrophages are derived from blood monocytes. They are able to ingest material by both phagocytic and pinocytic pathways.

MICROBIOLOGY

The answers and teaching notes to this section start on page 59.

93. The following statements relating to syphilis are correct:

☐ A *Treponema pallidum* is a Gram-negative organism
☐ B the primary chancre usually appears within one week of exposure to infection
☐ C spirochaetes are distributed throughout the body at the time of appearance of the primary chancre
☐ D serology is positive in all cases of tertiary syphilis
☐ E the Wasserman reaction (WR) is specific for syphilis

94. Cytomegalovirus

☐ A has infected over 60% of the adult population
☐ B is demonstrable in 0.5 to 1.5% of neonates
☐ C is an adenovirus
☐ D causes neonatal jaundice
☐ E is commonly present in the salivary glands

95. *Clostridia* organisms

☐ A are primarily saprophytic
☐ B are aerobic
☐ C undergo spore formation
☐ D produce endotoxins
☐ E are typically Gram-negative

96. *Treponema pallidum*

☐ A can be identified by direct light microscopy
☐ B can be cultured on a laboratory medium
☐ C is easily distinguished morphologically from *Treponema pertenue*
☐ D does not cause a true infection in any animal except man
☐ E crosses the human placenta

97. The following organisms commonly cause acute meningitis:

- [ ] A *Haemophilus influenzae*
- [ ] B *Neisseria meningitidis*
- [ ] C Beta haemolytic streptococcus
- [ ] D *Staphylococcus albus*
- [ ] E *Diplococcus pneumoniae*

98. In human immunodeficiency virus infection (HIV)

- [ ] A median time to progression to AIDS is five years
- [ ] B T-helper cells are especially susceptible
- [ ] C infected cells carry the CD5 molecule
- [ ] D the incubation period for HIV-1 is twice as long as for HIV-2
- [ ] E herpes simplex is a common infection

99. Tuberculosis

- [ ] A is now an uncommon disease
- [ ] B may be caused by *M. bovis*
- [ ] C may lead to meningitis
- [ ] D infection is suggested by a positive Wasserman reaction
- [ ] E is one of the commonest manifestations of AIDS

100. Rubella infection

- [ ] A is spread by direct contact
- [ ] B has an incubation period of 4 weeks
- [ ] C if acquired after the 16th week of pregnancy produces a congenital malformation in 30% of cases
- [ ] D specific IgM persists throughout the pregnancy
- [ ] E is caused by a rotavirus

101. Cytomegalovirus infection in pregnancy may cause the following in the fetus:

☐ A microcephaly
☐ B blood dyscrasias
☐ C myocarditis
☐ D pneumonia
☐ E enterocolitis

102. *Toxoplasma gondii*

☐ A is a virus
☐ B may be acquired by contact with cats
☐ C as a primary infection is uncommon during pregnancy
☐ D infection during pregnancy may cause purpura in the newborn
☐ E infection during pregnancy may cause choroidoretinitis in the infant

103. Bacteraemic shock

☐ A is caused by an exotoxin
☐ B may be associated with leukopenia
☐ C is usually caused by staphylococci
☐ D is improved by massive doses of steroids
☐ E is associated with sympathetic nervous activation

104. The following maternal infections may cause congenital infection in the neonate:

☐ A coxsackie B virus
☐ B cytomegalovirus
☐ C hepatitis B
☐ D poliomyelitis
☐ E herpes simplex (type 2)

105. Septicaemia

- ☐ A is commonly due to *Escherichia coli*
- ☐ B occurs in 20-30% of patients with gonococcal infection
- ☐ C leading to septic shock has a mortality rate of 20%
- ☐ D may be due to melioidosis
- ☐ E may lead to disseminated intravascular coagulation (DIC)

106. Which of the following are commonly due to *Staph. aureus*:

- ☐ A osteomyelitis
- ☐ B carbuncles
- ☐ C gastroenteritis
- ☐ D perinephric abscesses
- ☐ E sore throat

107. Candidiasis

- ☐ A is due to *Candida albicans*
- ☐ B stains Gram-negative
- ☐ C growth is optimal in alkaline conditions
- ☐ D may lead to septicaemia
- ☐ E may cause balanoposthitis

108. In the following diseases there is an animal reservoir of infection:

- ☐ A bubonic plague
- ☐ B diphtheria
- ☐ C anthrax
- ☐ D brucellosis
- ☐ E leptospirosis

93. **C**

T. pallidum cannot be Gram-stained but can be demonstrated by a silver impregnation method. The primary chancre appears 9-90 days following infection. In tertiary syphilis 10-20% of cases give negative reactions. The WR test is not specific for syphilis; yaws, pinta and bejel give positive reactions and false-positive reactions may occur in malaria, leprosy, glandular fever, smallpox vaccination and pregnancy. The treponemal immobilisation test is more reliable, but technically difficult. A living suspension of *T. pallidum* is incubated under anaerobic conditions in the presence of complement and patient's serum and observed under dark-ground illumination, where the spirochaetes are rendered non-motile, in positive cases.

94. **A B D E**

Cytomegalovirus is a herpes virus, a group that also includes herpes simplex virus and varicella. At least 80% of adults have been infected, and the proportion may be as high as 95%. Most are asymptomatic, but latent infection may occur, especially in salivary glands. Infection in utero may lead to cytomegalic inclusion disease, a fatal generalised illness characterised by jaundice, haemolysis and hepatosplenomegaly.

95. **A C D**

The *Clostridia* organisms consist of anaerobic Gram-positive bacilli which form spores that, in most cases, distend their bodies. They are widely distributed in nature as soil saprophytes and intestinal commensals of mammals. They include the causative organisms of botulism, tetanus, gas-gangrene and several intestinal infections. Their actions are typically mediated by endotoxins such as the powerful neurotoxin of *Clostridium tetani*.

96. **D E**

Treponema pallidum is purely a pathogenic parasite of man except under experimental conditions in apes, monkeys and rabbits. It is transmitted across the human placenta and thereby causes congenital syphilis. Being difficult to stain and of low refractibility it is best seen by dark-ground microscopy. It cannot easily be grown on laboratory cultures. Yaws is caused by *T. pertenue* which is indistinguishable from *T. pallidum* in morphology, in serological reactions and in response to treatment.

97. **A B E**

Whenever 'commonly' features in the stem of a question this presents difficulty as you have to ask yourself what is meant by the term. It is rather imprecise and really should not feature in MCQ questions. Nevertheless such questions will appear from time to time and it is true to say that the three organisms which are 'common' pathogens in the aetiology of acute meningitis are encountered relatively frequently. Nevertheless, it is a poor question!

98. **B E**

The median time to progression to full-blown AIDS is eight years. Infected cells carry the CD4 molecule. The incubation period for HIV-2 is substantially longer than for HIV-1.

99. **B C E**

Tuberculosis world-wide is very common, especially in Africa and Asia, but it is increasing in incidence in this country. The commonest organism is *Mycobacterium tuberculosis* but *M. bovis* may be ingested in milk and lead to lymph node involvement. The test used to investigate the possibility of infection is the Tuberculin test, strong positivity suggesting recent infection. It is very common in immuno-compromised patients, particularly those suffering from AIDS.

100. **D**

Rubella is caused by a togavirus and is spread mainly by the airborne route, and is highly transmissible. It has an incubation period of 2 to 3 weeks. Congenital rubella may lead to deafness and heart defects particularly, but infection after 16 weeks is not associated with the rubella syndrome.

101. **A B D**

Primary cytomegalovirus infection during pregnancy may affect both the placenta and the fetus in up to 50% of cases. The prognosis of the infection in the fetus is not known accurately, but it is thought that such infection may produce microcephaly, choroidoretinitis, eighth nerve damage, pneumonia, hepatosplenomegaly, anaemia (sometimes haemolytic with jaundice) and intrauterine growth retardation. Myocarditis and enterocolitis are not usually associated with CMV infection.

102. **B C D E**

Toxoplasma gondii is the protozoan parasite responsible for toxoplasmosis. The life cycle of the parasite involves the domestic cat. The risk of contracting the illness in the UK is small (estimated as less than 0.2% in recent surveys) but higher in France (6%). Fetal involvement appears greater the earlier in pregnancy the infection occurs. The common fetal manifestations are growth retardation, hepatosplenomegaly, jaundice, anaemia, petechiae, retinopathy, hydrocephaly and convulsions. Choroidoretinitis and intracranial calcification may not develop for several months after birth.

103. **B D E**

The clinical effects of bacteraemic shock result from absorbed endotoxins usually from Gram-negative organisms including *E. coli*, *Bacillus proteus* and *Klebsiella aerogenes*. Toxic damage to blood vessel walls leads to a loss of circulating fluid and protein into the extravascular space and a leukopenia is common. Massive doses of steroids may be helpful in reducing the passage of fluid and cells across capillary walls and also by sensitising arterioles to the effects of circulating noradrenaline and thereby maintaining blood pressure.

104. **A B C D E**

Coxsackie B virus infection, associated with Bornholm disease, but often unrecognised in the mother, may be transmitted to the fetus and give rise to a myocarditis or meningoencephalitis in the neonate; it has also been implicated as a possible cause of structural congenital heart disease and orogenital abnormalities.

Cytomegalovirus also is often asymptomatic in the mother and may be transmitted to the fetus or neonate transplacentally, or during passage through the birth canal, or during breast feeding. Infection in pregnancy may be associated with increased rate of abortion or premature delivery. Those infants born alive may be of low birth weight and may suffer fulminating disease in the neonatal period, with jaundice, thrombocytopenic purpura and choroidoretinitis. Chronic infection may be associated with spasticity, microcephaly and mental retardation.

Hepatitis B may be transmitted transplacentally and is associated with neonatal hepatitis.

Pregnant women show an increased susceptibility, severity and mortality from poliomyelitis; the fetus may be infected leading to intrauterine fetal death or neonatal paralysis.

Transplacental passage of herpes virus type 2 is uncommon although the infant may become infected during passage through the birth canal and develop a fatal disseminated infection.

105. **A D E**

Septicaemia complicates 1% of gonococcal infections. The mortality rate of septicaemia may be as high as 50%. Melioidosis is a rare infection due to *Pseudomonas pseudomallei* a saprophytic bacillus in certain soils and waters mainly in south-east Asia causing suppurative diseases which often resemble pulmonary tuberculosis.

106. **A B D**

Gastroenteritis is not caused by *Staph. aureus*, but by *E. coli*, *Shigella* etc. Sore throat is due usually to streptococcal infection.

107. **A D E**

Candidiasis is due to a Gram-positive organism and growth is optimal in acid conditions, hence its propensity to flourish in the vagina, especially during pregnancy. It may lead to balanoposthitis in the male, hence the need to treat both the male and female partner.

108. **A C D E**

The causative organism of bubonic plague, *Yersinia pestis*, is a flea-borne pathogen of rats and other rodents. *Corynebacterium diphtheriae* is an obligate parasite and man is its only natural host; it is not naturally pathogenic to animals. *Bacillus anthracis* is mainly a pathogen of herbivorous animals such as cattle, sheep, goats, horses and camels. Human infection is usually cutaneous by direct contact with infected animal products or a severe haemorrhagic infection of the bronchi and lungs acquired by inhalation. Brucella organisms which cause undulant fever in man are primarily pathogenic to goats, cattle and pigs. Many of the leptospira are pathogens of animals such as rats, mice, dogs, cattle and pigs from which human infection originates.

PATHOLOGY

The answers and teaching notes to this section start on page 68.

109. The following tumours arise in the ovary:

- ☐ A nephroblastoma
- ☐ B cystadenoma
- ☐ C granulosa cell tumour
- ☐ D neuroblastoma
- ☐ E teratoma

110. The following tumours are benign:

- ☐ A papilloma
- ☐ B seminoma
- ☐ C fibroma
- ☐ D multiple myeloma
- ☐ E neurofibroma

111. Ectopic pregnancy

- ☐ A occurs most commonly in the ovary
- ☐ B may lead to haemoperitoneum
- ☐ C may produce Arias-Stella changes in the endometrium
- ☐ D is associated with chronic salpingitis
- ☐ E can proceed to term

112. Squamous metaplasia

- ☐ A is a form of carcinoma in situ
- ☐ B may follow malignant change
- ☐ C occurs in the bladder
- ☐ D occurs in the urethra
- ☐ E occurs in the bronchial epithelium of cigarette smokers

113. Histological features of sarcoidosis include

- ☐ A epithelioid cells
- ☐ B caseation
- ☐ C round cell infiltration
- ☐ D Langhan's giant cells
- ☐ E Schaumann bodies

114. Features of benign tumours usually include:

- ☐ A an intact capsule
- ☐ B local invasion
- ☐ C well differentiated cell types
- ☐ D pleomorphism
- ☐ E regional lymphadenopathy

115. Adenocarcinoma of the cervix

- ☐ A constitutes 4-5% of cervical carcinomas
- ☐ B is less radiosensitive than squamous carcinomas
- ☐ C is characterised by intracellular mucin production
- ☐ D may be preceded by adenocarcinoma-in-situ
- ☐ E is rarely found in patients under 40 years of age

116. Vulvar intraepithelial neoplasia (VIN)

- ☐ A is usually found in patients over 60 years of age
- ☐ B is often asymptomatic
- ☐ C progresses to invasive carcinoma if untreated
- ☐ D is characterised by blunting of rete ridges in the epidermis
- ☐ E is associated with an increased risk of cervical intraepithelial neoplasia

117. Endometriosis

- ☐ A is characterised by the presence of ectopic endometrium
- ☐ B may turn malignant
- ☐ C more commonly affects the left side of the pelvis
- ☐ D affecting the ovary is known as adenomyosis
- ☐ E is more common in nullipara

118. Fibroadenomas of the breast

- ☐ A are relatively rare
- ☐ B have a peak incidence in the fifth decade of life
- ☐ C are usually multiple
- ☐ D may grow rapidly during pregnancy
- ☐ E may be diagnosed by fine-needle aspiration cytology

119. Breast carcinoma

- ☐ A is more common in nullipara
- ☐ B is most commonly found in the lower outer quadrant of the breast
- ☐ C has a better prognosis if tubular, rather than ductal, type
- ☐ D has a better prognosis if it contains oestrogen receptors
- ☐ E may be associated with microcalcification

120. Granulosa cell tumours of the ovary

- ☐ A are more common in post-menopausal than pre-menopausal women
- ☐ B are always unilateral
- ☐ C are characterised by the presence of Call-Exner bodies
- ☐ D may lead to endometrial carcinoma in 40-50% of patients
- ☐ E in juveniles carry a poor prognosis

121. Choriocarcinoma

- ☐ A is preceded by hydatidiform mole in 10% of cases
- ☐ B has a poor prognosis if associated with urinary HCG greater than 10,000 IU per 24 hours
- ☐ C may follow ectopic pregnancy
- ☐ D contains both syncitio- and cytotrophoblast
- ☐ E chorionic villi may be present

122. Malignant mixed mesodermal tumours of the uterus

- ☐ A contain both epithelial and mesodermal elements
- ☐ B constitute 10 to 15% of malignant tumours of the uterus
- ☐ C usually affect pre-menopausal women
- ☐ D carry a more favourable prognosis than endometrial carcinoma
- ☐ E may be diagnosed using periodic-acid-Schiff (PAS) stain

123. Granulation tissue

- ☐ A is a feature of wound healing
- ☐ B is present in the wall of an abscess
- ☐ C forms the capsule of a leiomyoma
- ☐ D leads to scar tissue formation
- ☐ E is a feature of amyloidosis

124. Macrophages

- ☐ A are derived from blood monocytes
- ☐ B are phagocytic
- ☐ C produce cellular antibodies
- ☐ D play an essential role in coagulation
- ☐ E can fuse to form giant cells

125. Increased capillary permeability in acute inflammation is produced by

- [ ] A histamine
- [ ] B bradykinin
- [ ] C angiotensin
- [ ] D 5-hydroxytryptamine
- [ ] E prostacyclin

126. In obstructive jaundice

- [ ] A plasma levels of conjugated bilirubin are normal
- [ ] B there is an increased amount of stercobilinogen in the faeces
- [ ] C there is an increased amount of urobilinogen in the urine
- [ ] D bilirubin is present in the urine
- [ ] E there is increased hepatic production of alakaline phosphatase

127. Phenylketonuria

- [ ] A may be detected using the Guthrie test
- [ ] B is due to a deficiency of phenylalanine hydroxylase
- [ ] C is characterised by hyperpigmentation of the skin
- [ ] D occurs in 1 in 1000 infants in Britain
- [ ] E is characterised by mental retardation

128. Congenital adrenal hyperplasia is associated with

- [ ] A stillbirth
- [ ] B precocious pseudopuberty in male infants
- [ ] C symptoms and signs of salt loss
- [ ] D neonatal jaundice
- [ ] E ambiguous genitalia in the newborn

109. B C E

The cystadenoma, granulosa cell tumour and teratoma may all occur in the ovary, being derived from neoplastic growth in epithelial, sex cord and germ cell structures respectively.

The nephroblastoma and neuroblastoma are developmental tumours of kidney and nerve tissue respectively, occurring almost exclusively in early childhood and showing a sarcomatous appearance.

110. A C E

A papilloma is a benign epithelial tumour the cells of which cover finger-like processes of stroma. A fibroma is a benign connective tissue tumour made up of fibroblasts and collagen fibres in varying proportion. A neurofibroma is a benign fibrous tumour of the endoneurium of cutaneous or deeper nerve trunks; the cutaneous form may be multiple (von Recklinghausen's disease) and both forms may progress to sarcomatous change.

The seminoma is a malignant testicular tumour, of seminiferous tubules. Multiple myeloma is a malignant tumour of bone marrow affecting specifically the plasma cells.

111. B C D E

The Fallopian tube is the commonest site for ectopic pregnancy. The presence of Arias-Stella change in the endometrium without chorionic villi or fetal parts raises the possibility of ectopic pregnancy. Chronic salpingitis may damage the tubal epithelium, particularly the ciliated cells which facilitate ovum transport along the tube. Although an ectopic pregnancy may proceed to term, this is very rare with the fetus usually attaching itself to the bowel mesentary or abdominal wall and gaining a blood supply from this source.

112. B C D E

Metaplasia is the transformation of one type of tissue into another; as such it usually represents a response to a call for altered function or is the result of an altered environment. This process is in marked contrast to anaplasia which represents the reversion of a more highly to a less highly differentiated tissue. Metaplasia is not a form of in situ malignant change. Squamous metaplasia may occur in the bladder or endometrium especially in response to changes in oestrogen status and in the cervix, when the endocervical glandular epithelium becomes exposed to the low pH of the vagina. Ciliated glandular epithelium in cigarette smokers may undergo metaplasia to squamous epithelium.

113. A D E

Sarcoidosis is a systemic disease of uncertain aetiology, characterised histologically by epithelioid cells in a discrete follicle. Schaumann bodies refer to spherical basophilic masses in Langhan's giant cells, which may be found amongst the epithelioid cells. Unlike the tubercle follicle, there is never any true caseation and no round cell infiltration.

114. A C

Local invasion or distant metastases to regional lymph nodes are characteristic features of malignancy. Pleomorphism which is the marked difference in size, shape and other morphological features of cells is seen in dysplastic or anaplastic cells and is therefore more likely to indicate malignancy. An intact capsule and well differentiated histology are common features of benign tumours.

115. C D

Adenocarcinoma of the cervix is increasing in incidence relative to squamous carcinomas and now may constitute over 20% of cervical carcinomas. There is a suggestion that the two varieties arise from common 'stem cells' and that they should perhaps be considered as one disease. Many cervical adenocarcinomas exhibit intracellular mucin (but not necessarily the poorly differentiated varieties) and this helps to distinguish them from endometrial carcinomas. Adenocarcinoma of the cervix is equally radiosensitive to squamous carcinomas and is not uncommon in women under 40 years of age. Adenocarcinoma-in-situ is thought to predispose to invasive carcinoma.

116. E

Vulvar intraepithelial neoplasia is a rare condition which often affects younger women (and children occasionally). It usually leads to symptoms, especially pruritus vulvae. There is no convincing evidence of progression to invasion, especially as the peak incidence for invasive carcinoma is in the sixth to seventh decades of life. Loss of rete ridges is characteristic of lichen sclerosus.

The term 'vulvar dystrophy' should no longer be used. Instead, vulvar abnormalities should be divided into neoplastic and non-neoplastic epithelial disorders (NNED). The former include VIN and invasive carcinoma of the vulva whereas NNED include lichen sclerosus, squamous hyperplasia and generalised dermatoses affecting the vulva.

117. A B E

Endometriosis may rarely turn malignant, especially when affecting the ovary (clear cell carcinoma). Adenomyosis describes endometriosis affecting the myometrium and is more common in nullipara, when it may contribute to infertility.

118. D E

Fibroadenomas are the commonest benign tumours of the breast and have a peak incidence during the third decade of life. Normally they are solitary lesions but can occasionally be multiple. They are hormone sensitive and may grow rapidly during pregnancy. Fine-needle aspiration cytology is useful in distinguishing fibroadenomas from malignant lesions, but trucut biopsy may be necessary to make a definitive diagnosis.

119. A C D E

Breast cancer is more common in nullipara; it has been suggested that if first pregnancy is delayed until age 30, the risk of breast cancer is increased over those who have first pregnancy earlier. If there is also a strong family history the risk of breast cancer may be as high as 1 in 8. The most common site is the upper outer quadrant (50% of tumours). Only about 10% of breast carcinomas occur in the lower outer quadrant. Tubular carcinoma has a significantly more favourable prognosis than the more common ductal type. Oestrogen receptor positivity is associated with a better prognosis, as it is often associated with better differentiation and there is often a good response to hormone therapy. Microcalcification forms the basis of mammographic screening.

120. A C

Granulosa cell tumours are more common in postmenopausal than premenopausal women, but 5% are diagnosed before the age of normal puberty and most of these are associated with isosexual precocity, accounting for 10% of the cases of that syndrome in the female.

Granulosa cell tumours are unilateral in over 95% of cases. They are characterised by Call-Exner bodies which are multiple small cavities containing eosinophilic fluid and often a few degenerating nuclei. Granulosa cell tumours secrete oestrogen and this may stimulate the endometrium to develop simple hyperplasia, adenomatous hyperplasia and in approximately 5% of cases, adenocarcinoma. Some series however, report incidences of 25%. Juvenile tumours generally have a more malignant appearance than other forms, they appear to be associated with a good prognosis and therefore conservative treatment may be appropriate.

121. C D
Choriocarcinoma is preceded by hydatidiform mole in 30% to 50% of cases. A urinary HCG excretion of greater than 100,000 IU per 24 hours is an unfavourable prognostic factor along with duration of disease prior to chemotherapy greater than four months, metastases to brain or liver, and prior unsuccessful chemotherapy. It may follow ectopic pregnancy and contains both syncitio- and cytotrophoblast. Chorionic villi are absent.

122. A E
Malignant mixed mesodermal tumours of the ovary are rare, constituting less than 1.5% of malignant tumours of the uterus. Most patients are post-menopausal, the median age ranging between 62 and 68 years. They carry a poor prognosis. PAS stain may be helpful in staining the glycogen in rhabdomyoblasts.

123. A B D
See answer to question 44, practice examination 1.

124. A B E
There are two major groups of phagocytic cells, the polymorphonuclear leucocytes of the blood, or microphages and the mononuclear cells or macrophages. The latter may either circulate in the blood, when they are called monocytes, or may be fixed in the tissues, in which case they are called histiocytes; it is now established that tissue macrophages are derived from peripheral blood monocytes. It was previously assumed that macrophages were antibody producers, but there is now good evidence that instead they act as antibody processing and presenting cells, which 'instruct' antibody production

by lymphocytes. Macrophages may coalesce to form giant cells e.g. the fusion of epithelioid cells to form Langhan's cells in tuberculosis. They play no part in the coagulation process.

125. A B D E

Histamine is a vasoactive substance, particularly important in the early stages of acute inflammation. It causes contraction of extravascular smooth muscle, dilatation of blood vessels and increases capillary permeability. 5-hydroxytryptamine, or serotonin, is released from mast cells and plays a similar role to histamine. Bradykinin causes smooth muscle contraction but more slowly than histamine. It also vasodilates and is the most powerful active permeability factor known, in addition to producing pain. Prostacyclin, (PGI 2) which is produced by the endothelial cells of blood vessels, causes vasodilatation and increases permeability. Angiotensin reduces capillary permeability.

126. D E

When there is obstruction to the flow of bile, either intra- or extra-hepatically, the process of conjugation of bilirubin by the hepatocytes will initially proceed normally. Conjugated bilirubin, therefore, no longer excreted via the bile ducts, accumulates in the plasma. This is a relatively small molecule, since it is not protein bound and is therefore readily excreted in urine. Since the flow of conjugated bilirubin down the bile duct is interrupted, the production of stercobilinogen by intestinal bacteria is reduced and this along with its oxidation product stercobilin is present in reduced amount in faeces. The reabsorption and enterohepatic circulation of these pigments is also therefore reduced and their excretion in urine as urobilinogen and urobilin decreases.

It is not clear how plasma alkaline phosphatase levels relate to hepatic excretory function but their determination is of value in the jaundiced patient. In post-hepatic (obstructive) jaundice, levels rise markedly; in hepatic jaundice the elevation is usually of lesser degree and in pre-hepatic (haemolytic) jaundice levels usually remain normal.

127. A B E

The Guthrie test is performed as a routine screening test on all neonates using blood obtained from a heel prick and phenylketonuria is an enzyme deficiency. Hypopigmentation is the characteristic feature.

Phenylketonuria occurs at a rate of about 1 in 10,000 infants. Mental retardation results from damage by toxic metabolites of phenylalanine.

128. **B C E**
Congenital adrenal hyperplasia, most commonly due to 21-hydroxylase deficiency causes increased synthesis of androgens leading to ambiguous genitalia in female neonates and precocious pseudo-puberty in male infants. Because of the defective synthesis of aldosterone, sodium loss occurs. The basic defect is a block of aldosterone and cortisol synthesis with precursors being diverted to the synthesis of androgens.

PHARMACOLOGY

The answers and teaching notes to this section start on page 78.

129. Propranolol

- [ ] A is an alpha-adrenoceptor antagonist (alpha blocker)
- [ ] B leads to membrane stabilisation
- [ ] C has partial agonist activity
- [ ] D has high lipid solubility
- [ ] E use may mask hypoglycaemia in diabetics

130. Oral contraceptives

- [ ] A inhibit release of gonadotrophic hormones
- [ ] B may lead to thinning of cervical mucus
- [ ] C may influence Fallopian tube smooth muscle activity
- [ ] D lead to reduced platelet aggregation
- [ ] E lead to increased antithrombin III

131. Heparin

- [ ] A may be administered orally
- [ ] B is metabolised chiefly in the kidney
- [ ] C has low plasma protein binding affinity
- [ ] D acts on activated factor XII
- [ ] E control is measured by activated partial thromboplastin time

132. Warfarin

- [ ] A does not cross the placenta
- [ ] B is metabolised chiefly in the liver
- [ ] C acts eight to twelve hours following administration
- [ ] D interferes with production of factor VI
- [ ] E control is based on prothrombin time

133. Prostaglandins

- ☐ A are small molecular weight polypeptides
- ☐ B are chemically related to thromboxanes
- ☐ C have been shown clearly to be responsible for luteolysis in man
- ☐ D inhibit secretion of renin
- ☐ E are produced in the seminal vesicles of man

134. The following cytotoxic drugs are alkylating agents:

- ☐ A anthracycline
- ☐ B chlorambucil
- ☐ C 6-mercaptopurine
- ☐ D cyclophosphamide
- ☐ E vinblastine

135. Morphine

- ☐ A increases the concentration of alveolar pCO_2
- ☐ B dilates the pupils in man
- ☐ C causes orthostatic hypotension
- ☐ D causes a rise in intrabiliary duct pressure
- ☐ E is mainly excreted by the kidney

136. The following drugs cross the placental barrier:

- ☐ A heparin
- ☐ B tetracycline
- ☐ C sulphadimidine
- ☐ D diazepam
- ☐ E salicylate

137. Hydrocortisone

- [ ] A causes eosinophilia
- [ ] B increases urinary calcium excretion
- [ ] C causes negative nitrogen balance
- [ ] D decreases urinary potassium excretion
- [ ] E decreases gluconeogenesis

138. Vitamin C is

- [ ] A found only in animal foodstuffs
- [ ] B necessary for wound healing
- [ ] C fat soluble
- [ ] D rapidly destroyed by heating
- [ ] E preserved by food freezing

139. Bromocriptine

- [ ] A is a derivative of ergot
- [ ] B is a vasoconstrictor
- [ ] C inhibits prolactin secretion at the pituitary level
- [ ] D is teratogenic
- [ ] E causes raised prolactin levels to return to normal after 48-72 hours of treatment

140. Atropine

- [ ] A dries bronchial and salivary secretions
- [ ] B is used to avoid unwanted effects of neostigmine
- [ ] C diminishes the risk of vagal cardiac arrest
- [ ] D leads to loss of accommodation in the eye
- [ ] E may produce allergy in the eye

129. **B D E**

Propranolol is a beta-blocker with high lipid solubility. It produces membrane stabilisation which may be useful in the treatment of cardiac dysrhythmias, in high dosage. It has no partial agonist activity. When a diabetic takes insulin the lowering of blood sugar is opposed by liver and muscle glycogenolysis, which are predominantly beta-sympathetic actions. If beta-blockers are present there may be a phase of insulin hypoglycaemia unannounced by the typically sympathetically mediated symptoms of tachycardia or tremor.

130. **A C**

Oral contraceptives inhibit release of gonadotrophic hormones, hence prevent ovulation. They lead to thickening of the cervical mucus and may either increase Fallopian tube activity (high doses of oestrogen) or reduce it (progesterone-only preparations lead to a slightly increased risk of ectopic pregnancy). There is increased platelet aggregation and decreased antithrombin II activity, hence a slightly increased risk of thromboembolism.

131. **D E**

Heparin is given intravenously or subcutaneously; it is inactivated following oral administration. It is metabolised chiefly in the liver and has a high plasma protein binding affinity. It acts chiefly as an antithrombin but does have activity against activated factors IX, X, XI and XII.

132. **B E**

Warfarin crosses the placenta and should not be given if delivery is thought to be imminent. Heparin is of high molecular weight and does not cross the placenta. It takes 24 to 72 hours to work and is taken orally. It interferes with production of factors II, VII, IX and X.

133. **B E**

Prostaglandins are produced in the seminal vesicles of man, but also in other tissues such as kidney, lung and brain. They are modified hydroxyacids derived from prostanoic acid and contain a cyclopentane ring. They are related chemically to the thromboxanes. Prostaglandins of the E series increase renin secretion. There is no conclusive evidence that they are responsible for luteolysis in man; the evidence is speculative therefore the answer must be false.

134. B D

Chlorambucil and cyclophosphamide are alkylating agents; they interact with DNA. Anthracycline is an antibiotic. 6-mercaptopurine is an antimetabolite, whose mode of action is to interfere with nucleic acid syntheses. Vinblastine (a vinca alkaloid) arrests cells in metaphase of mitosis.

135. A C D E

Morphine depresses respiration by reducing sensitivity of the respiratory centre to rises in blood carbon dioxide tension; with high doses carbon dioxide narcosis may develop. The pupils constrict (due to third nerve muscle stimulation). Morphine impairs sympathetic vascular reflexes and stimulates the vagal centre. Orthostatic hypotension may therefore be a problem, particularly in those taking antihypertensive drugs. Intrabiliary pressure may rise substantially, due to spasm of the sphincter of Oddi; biliary colic may therefore be aggravated by morphine. Morphine is conjugated in the liver (glucuronide) and excreted by the kidney.

136. B C D E

Tetracycline is contraindicated in pregnancy because it does cross the placenta and may lead to deposition in and staining of deciduous teeth and bones, tooth malformations and decrease in linear bone growth. Sulphadimidine rapidly crosses the placenta from mother to fetus. If given immediately prior to delivery there is a theoretical risk of competition between sulphonamides and bilirubin for binding sites on neonatal albumin. Diazepam readily crosses the placenta whichever route of administration is used and can cause behavioural problems for many hours after birth if given in late pregnancy or labour. Salicylates cross the placenta and cause neonatal platelet dysfunction, decreased neonatal factor XII, neonatal haemorrhage and respiratory distress syndrome.

137. B C

Glucocorticoids, of which hydrocortisone (cortisol) is one, decrease the number of circulating eosinophils by increasing their sequestration in the spleen and lungs. They increase protein catabolism and increase hepatic glycogenesis and gluconeogenesis. Glucose-6-phosphatase activity is increased and the blood glucose rises. In excessive amounts, such as is seen in Cushing's syndrome, glucocorticoids lead to bone dissolution, elevated glomerular filtration rate and increased calcium excretion. In addition, significant potassium depletion may result from increased excretion.

138. B D E

Ascorbic acid is a water-soluble vitamin found in citrus fruits and green vegetables; milk and meat contain only traces. Vitamin C is easily destroyed by oxidation at moderate temperatures; consequently large losses occur in cooking. Freezing of food does not disrupt vitamin C. The vitamin serves a vital role in collagen synthesis and wound healing.

139. A B C

Bromocryptine is a semisynthetic ergot alkaloid. It is rapidly and extensively absorbed from the gastrointestinal tract. Its peak plasma concentration occurs 2-3 hours following ingestion. A single dose is able to suppress prolactin levels within 3-4 hours and its action will continue for 8-12 hours. Bromocryptine is a dopamine agonist, believed to act directly on the dopamine receptors in the prolactin secreting cells of the pituitary gland. It is a vasoconstrictor and therefore should not be used in patients with coronary vascular or peripheral vascular disease. Bromocryptine has been widely used in the treatment of infertility and there is no evidence that it is teratogenic.

140. A B C D E

Atropine blocks muscarinic acetylcholine receptors. It is used with neostigmine in anaesthesia to offset the muscarinic side-effects of the latter. It is useful in anaesthesia to diminish the risk of vagal cardiac arrest and to combat bradycardia.

The answers and teaching notes to this section start on page 86.

141. During pregnancy

- ☐ A glycosuria is an effective test of carbohydrate intolerance
- ☐ B fasting plasma glucose concentration is decreased
- ☐ C fasting plasma insulin concentration is decreased
- ☐ D the oral glucose tolerance test alters with advancing gestation
- ☐ E two hours after an oral glucose load, plasma insulin concentration should have returned to normal

142. The amnion

- ☐ A is surrounded by the chorion
- ☐ B is derived from the blastocyst
- ☐ C in a dizygous (binovular) twin pregnancy is separated from its fellow by the chorion
- ☐ D covers the fetal surface of the placenta
- ☐ E separates from the decidua in the third stage of labour

143. The following statements relating to the histology of the skin are correct:

- ☐ A apocrine sweat glands are the most common in man
- ☐ B the arrectores pili muscles contribute to sebum release
- ☐ C in split-skin grafts only half of the thickness of the epidermis is removed
- ☐ D melanocytes synthesise the enzyme tyrosinase
- ☐ E corpuscles of Ruffini are receptors for touch

144. Fetal heart rate

- ☐ A varies with gestational age
- ☐ B is not subject to parasympathetic activity before the 20th week of pregnancy
- ☐ C may accelerate with external head compression
- ☐ D increases as maternal temperature rises
- ☐ E accelerates in response to maternal ingestion of atropine sulphate

145. During the normal menstrual cycle

☐ A oestrogen is predominant during the proliferative phase
☐ B menstrual blood loss averages 150 ml
☐ C cervical mucus becomes more viscous at the time of ovulation
☐ D menstruation is preceded by a rise in plasma progesterone levels
☐ E menstruation is associated with dilatation of the basal segment of the spiral arteries within the endometrium

146. Renal blood flow

☐ A accounts for 10-15% of cardiac output
☐ B may be estimated from creatinine clearance
☐ C largely passes to the renal medulla
☐ D decreases during exercise
☐ E increases during pregnancy

147. Cardiac output

☐ A is approximately 4 litres in a pregnant woman
☐ B can increase fivefold during exercise
☐ C increases with an increase in aortic pressure
☐ D decreases on exposure to positive gravity
☐ E increases in response to increased heart rate

148. Fetal respiratory movements in utero

☐ A are normally present for 80% of the 24 hour period
☐ B occur at a frequency of two per minute
☐ C are increased in asymmetrical growth retardation
☐ D are reduced after maternal meals
☐ E increase with increasing gestation

149. In the human, fertilisation normally occurs

☐ A in the ampullary region of the Fallopian tube
☐ B after extrusion of the first polar body
☐ C within 48 hours of ovulation
☐ D 14 days before implantation
☐ E in the presence of cervical mucus ferning

150. Ovulation occurs

- ☐ A before the triphasic rise in temperature
- ☐ B before the LH (luteinising hormone) surge
- ☐ C following follicular ripening by FSH (follicle stimulating hormone)
- ☐ D infrequently in women with amenorrhoea
- ☐ E after the disappearance of cervical mucus ferning

151. Trophoblast

- ☐ A enters the maternal circulation in normal pregnancy
- ☐ B is lysed in the maternal lung
- ☐ C is genetically maternal
- ☐ D produces human chorionic gonadotrophin
- ☐ E is immunologically inert

152. The increased uterine blood flow in pregnancy is contributed to by

- ☐ A an increase in the number of uterine arterioles
- ☐ B increased diameter of placental blood vessels
- ☐ C reduced vascular resistance in the uterus
- ☐ D increased angiotensin II levels
- ☐ E increased blood volume

153. In renal function

- ☐ A glomerular filtration can be measured using inulin
- ☐ B changes in osmotic pressure can cause significant changes in glomerular filtration
- ☐ C carbonic anhydrase increases the rate of conversion of H_2CO_3 into H^+ and HCO_3^-
- ☐ D 90% of filtered water is reabsorbed
- ☐ E the ascending loop of Henle is relatively impermeable to water

154. Cardiac output

☐ A need not increase when the heart rate increases and is irregular
☐ B increases when the subject changes from the standing to the supine position
☐ C is commonly expressed as the combined outputs of both ventricles per minute
☐ D is increased reflexly in a hot climate
☐ E is the product of heart rate and stroke volume

155. A sustained arterial hypertension may be due to

☐ A excessive aldosterone secretion
☐ B left ventricular hypertrophy
☐ C excessive secretion of adrenocorticotrophic hormone
☐ D hypoxia consequent to chronic respiratory failure
☐ E drug therapy with methyl dopa

156. Total cerebral blood flow is most markedly increased by

☐ A hypercapnia
☐ B hypoxia
☐ C cerebral activity
☐ D vasomotor reflexes
☐ E increase in mean arterial pressure

157. Carbon dioxide is transported in the blood

☐ A in combination with haemoglobin
☐ B as hydrochloric acid
☐ C in combination with plasma proteins
☐ D mainly as bicarbonate
☐ E in physical solution in plasma

158. The respiratory centre

- [ ] A is situated in the medulla oblongata
- [ ] B is inhibited during vomiting
- [ ] C sends out regular impulses to the inspiratory muscles during quiet respiration
- [ ] D is reflexly regulated by vagal impulses
- [ ] E is sensitive to blood pH alterations

159. The following changes occur during normal pregnancy:

- [ ] A blood pressure tends to be elevated in the second trimester
- [ ] B cardiac output rises only during the second and third trimesters
- [ ] C heart rate rises by 20%
- [ ] D plasma volume rises by 40%
- [ ] E stroke volume is unchanged

160. Renal blood flow is

- [ ] A reduced during fear and emotional stress
- [ ] B unchanged by noradrenaline administration
- [ ] C greater per unit mass of tissue in the medulla than in the cortex
- [ ] D determined by the metabolic needs of the kidney
- [ ] E reduced when arterial pressure falls, by about the same percentage

141. B D

During pregnancy, fasting plasma glucose concentration is decreased, probably due to the haemodilution effect of the increased plasma volume. The glomerular filtration rate is increased in normal pregnancy; this may lead to the renal threshold being exceeded and to glycosuria without impaired glucose tolerance. Fasting plasma insulin concentration rises in late pregnancy to accompany the increased glucose requirements. Glucose tolerance alters during pregnancy; although plasma glucose levels should have returned to normal two hours after an oral glucose load, insulin concentration frequently remains elevated.

142. A B C D

The amnion is derived from the blastocyst and is surrounded by the chorion. It is separated from its fellow by the chorion in a dizygous twin pregnancy. If one chorion only is present, the pregnancy is monozygous. If a double chorion is present, the pregnancy may be either mono-, or dizygous. The amnion covers the fetal surface of the placenta. The chorion is in contact with the decidua and therefore separates during the third stage of labour.

143. B D

Exocrine glands are commonest; apocrine glands occur in axilla, pubic region and areolae of breasts. The arrectores pili muscles pass obliquely from the epidermis to the slanting surface of the hair follicles deep to the sebaceous glands. By contracting, they cause the hairs to stand erect and lead to the release of sebum. Split-skin grafts consist of epidermis, dermis and the superficial layers of the corium; regeneration takes place from hair follicles and sweat ducts. Melanocytes lie in the deepest layer of the epidermis. Melanin results from the enzymatic oxidation of tyrosine by tyrosinase, which is attached to the melanocytes at the epidermo-dermal junction. Corpuscles of Ruffini are thought to be heat receptors.

144. A B C D E

Basal fetal heart rate varies with gestational age, partly because it is not subject to parasympathetic activity before the 20th week of pregnancy. The heart rate may accelerate with external head compression although bradycardia is more usual. An uncomplicated tachycardia is often a sign of maternal pyrexia. Atropine sulphate, by causing parasympathetic blockade leads to acceleration of the maternal and fetal heart rate.

145. A

Oestrogen concentration in plasma increases during the proliferative phase of the menstrual cycle, to allow the development of the endometrium prior to ovulation (and possible implantation). It is produced under the influence of LH and transported to the granulosa cells, where it is aromatised to oestrone and oestradiol, the latter being the active steroid. It is also responsible for the secretion of clear mucus from the cervix which facilitates sperm penetration. Positive feedback allows the LH surge which leads to ovulation. Following ovulation the secretory phase of the cycle ensues, with secretion of both oestrogen and progesterone. The progesterone acts on oestrogen-primed tissues to produce a secretory endometrium and a thick cervical mucus. If fertilisation and blastocyst implantation do not occur then the corpus luteum begins to involute and steroid formation falls. The maintenance of the secretory epithelium is no longer possible, the spiral arteries collapse and the endometrium sloughs leading to bleeding. The average menstrual loss is only of the order of 30 ml but of course may be much more in cases of severe menorrhagia.

146. B D E

Renal blood flow is approximately 200 ml per minute which represents about 20% of the cardiac output. Blood flow is not homogeneous, the cortex being better perfused than the medulla, which receives only about 7-10% of the renal flow. This is important for the development of hyperosmolality of the inner medulla and a hypertonic urine. Blood flow may fall by 30-40% during exercise.

147. B D

Cardiac output is the product of stroke volume and heart rate. At rest the stroke volume is approximately 70 ml and the heart rate approximately 70 beats per minute, giving an output of 4.5 to 5 litres. It increases to approximately 6 litres during pregnancy. Increased heart rate does not necessarily result in increased cardiac output, as filling time and diastolic volume may be reduced. Aortic pressure is unlikely to influence cardiac output; venous return is much more significant. Exposure to positive gravity leads to pooling of blood in veins and reduced cardiac output.

148. E

Fetal breathing movements detected by real-time ultrasound occur with a frequency of 50-60 breaths per minute. The proportion of time that is spent in breathing movements increases with gestation from around 10% at 28 weeks to 50% at term. Breathing activities also show a diurnal variation with three distinct patterns of periodicity; increasing cyclically every 1-1.5 hours. Fetal breathing movements have also been found to occur for a reduced proportion of time in various disorders of pregnancy including growth retardation, antepartum haemorrhage and pre-eclampsia.

149. A B C E

During follicular development the first meiotic division, arrested in prophase during intrauterine development, is resumed about 36 hours prior to ovulation and is completed with the extrusion of the first polar body a few hours prior to ovulation. The second meiotic division proceeds as far as metaphase, to be completed only after fertilisation, which usually occurs in the ampullary region of the tube. The morula usually enters the uterus 3-5 days after fertilisation and shortly thereafter implantation occurs. Cervical mucus ferning, characteristic of oestrogen predominance, is usually lost within a short time after ovulation as progesterone secretion from the corpus luteum increases.

150. A C D

Ovarian activity in humans is cyclical, the production and release of oocytes by the ovary being episodic and coordinated with its endocrine activity. FSH is largely responsible for the growth of antral follicles to maturity. The LH surge causes changes in the follicle cells of the most advanced oocyte that result in the expulsion of the oocyte at ovulation. The period prior to ovulation is characterised by oestrogen dominance, after ovulation by progestogen and oestrogen together. Both rise in basal body temperature and the disappearance of cervical mucus ferning are attributed to the progesterone produced by the corpus luteum which forms after oocyte expulsion. Anovulation is one cause of amenorrhoea but the relationship is not absolute. Conversely regular menstruation does not necessarily indicate regular ovulation.

151. A B D

Trophoblast cells may be found in the decidus basilis and myometrium and it has been estimated that up to 10,000 clumps of cells may be released daily into the maternal circulation to be lysed in the lung. It was at one time suggested that syncytiotrophoblast may be derived from granulosa cells of the ovary, but there is now no doubt that it is fetal in origin. The endometrium constitutes a partial immunologically privileged site because of its limited lymphatic supply; this privilege is important since the trophoblast is not immunologically inert, but expresses HLA antigens, albeit in low levels. Syncytiotrophoblast secretes HCG in addition to HPL, Schwangershaft's protein (SP1), various other pregnancy-associated proteins and steroids.

152. **B C E**

Angiotensin II levels are increased in normal pregnancy, although vascular sensitivity is reduced and it is unlikely that this factor is of relevance to altered uterine blood flow. The most significant factors are the increased blood volume and reduced uterine vascular resistance resulting from dilatation of the arcuate arteries. The actual number of vessels does not change.

153. **A B D E**

Inulin is freely filtered through the glomeruli and is neither secreted nor reabsorbed by the tubules and therefore can be used to measure glomerular filtration rate. GFR is influenced by three factors: the size of the capillary bed; the permeability of the capillaries; and the hydrostatic and osmotic pressure gradients across the capillary wall. As osmotic pressure of the filtrate in the tubule is negligible, this latter gradient is equal to the osmotic pressure of the plasma in the glomerular capillaries. At least 90% of filtered water is normally reabsorbed; the remainder of the filtered water can be reabsorbed without affecting total solute excretion. The descending limb of the loop of Henle is permeable to water but the ascending limb is relatively impermeable. Acid secretion by the tubular cells of the kidney is facilitated by carbonic anhydrase which catalyses the reaction $CO_2 + H_2O = H_2CO_3$.

154. **A B D E**

Cardiac output is the output of the heart per unit time. It is calculated by the product of the stroke volume and heart rate in beats per minute. The stroke volume is the amount of blood pumped out of each ventricle per beat. In the resting person, in the supine position, the stroke volume will average 80 ml (the actual volume put out by the two ventricles in series will be twice the stroke volume, i.e. 80 ml from the left ventricle and 80 ml from the right). The cardiac output will usually increase when the heart rate increases but this is not true of rapid arrhythmias. Normal cardiac output will decrease on sitting or standing from the supine position and conversely will increase when the subject becomes supine after standing. A high environmental temperature will cause increased cardiac output via increased venous return.

155. A C D

Deoxycorticosterone and aldosterone elevate the blood pressure and hypertension is a prominent feature of primary hyperaldosteronism. Hypertension is also seen in Cushing's syndrome in which aldosterone secretion is usually normal. Although the cause in this syndrome is uncertain it may be that increased circulating ACTH (adreno-corticotrophic hormone) produces an increase in secretion of deoxycorticosterone. Hypertension is usually due to increased peripheral resistance which is likely to cause left ventricular hypertrophy rather than the converse. Chronic respiratory failure leads to pulmonary vasoconstriction and pulmonary hypertension but is unlikely to affect systemic blood pressure unless severe polycythaemia is produced. Alpha-methyl dopa is a drug which depresses sympathetic activity by forming a false transmitter and therefore causes peripheral vasodilatation and hypotension.

156. A B E

Total cerebral blood flow is generally maintained at a constant level under varying conditions. Although there are significant shifts in the pattern of flow, total cerebral flow is not increased by strenuous mental activity. Mean arterial pressure does not affect total cerebral blood flow positively. Changes in blood gas tensions affect cerebral blood flow positively. Changes in blood gas tensions affect cerebral arterioles; a low pO_2 is associated with vasodilatation while a rise in pCO_2 (hypercapnia) also exerts a potent dilator effect. Although cerebral vessels are innervated by noradrenergic vasoconstrictor fibres and cholinergic vasodilator fibres, vasomotor reflexes appear to play little if any part in the regulation of cerebral blood flow in humans.

157. **A C D E**

Carbon dioxide is transported in the blood, both in physical solution (5%) and in combined forms with haemoglobin, plasma proteins or bicarbonate (95%). The carbon dioxide that diffuses into red blood cells is rapidly hydrated to H_2CO_3 because of the presence of carbonic anhydrase. The H_2CO_3 dissociates to H^+ and HCO_3^-, the H^+ being buffered by haemoglobin. Since the HCO_3^- content of red cells is much greater than that of plasma, cell membranes being relatively impermeable to cation, much (around 70%) of the HCO_3^- diffuses out into the plasma, electrochemical neutrality is maintained by diffusion of Cl^- into the red cells (the so-called 'chloride shift'); CO_2 is not however transported as HCl in the blood. Some of the CO_2 in red cells reacts with the amino groups of proteins to form carbamino compounds. In the plasma, CO_2 also reacts with plasma proteins to form small amounts of carbamino compounds and small amounts are hydrated to H_2CO_3; this latter reaction is however slow in the absence of carbonic anhydrase. Most of the CO_2 in the plasma therefore is carried as bicarbonate whereas in erythrocytes the majority is carried as carbamino-haemoglobin.

158. **A B C D E**

Automatic spontaneous respiration is dependent upon nerve impulses from the pons and medulla causing discharge of motor neurones that innervate the respiratory muscles. This rhythmic discharge is modified by centres in the pons and by afferents in the vagus nerves arising from receptors in the lung parenchyma; stretching of the lungs during inspiration inhibits respiratory drive. An increase in pCO_2 or H^+ concentration or a decrease in pO_2 acts via chemoreceptors in the medulla, carotid and aortic bodies to stimulate respiratory centre activity. Inhibition of respiration and closure of the glottis prevent aspiration during swallowing, gagging and vomiting.

159. **C D**

In the normal pregnant woman at rest, but not lying supine, cardiac output rises from early pregnancy to a peak at around 20 weeks gestation which is approximately 1.5 litres per minute, or 40% above the non-pregnant level; this rise is maintained through the rest of pregnancy. This increase in cardiac output is achieved both by an increase in heart rate (averaging 15 beats per minute) and stroke volume (from 65 to 70 ml); again these changes are present from early pregnancy. The general pattern in blood pressure seen by most observers suggests relatively little change in systolic pressure, but a marked fall in diastolic pressure which is lowest in mid-pregnancy and thereafter rises to approximate non-pregnant levels again by term; for most of pregnancy therefore there is an increase in pulse pressure. Plasma volume changes vary with age, parity, race and 'reproductive performance'. In healthy women in their first pregnancy, plasma volume increases by about 40% over the non-pregnant level of 2600 ml, between 12 and 32 weeks' gestation.

160. A B

The blood flow in the renal cortex is much greater than in the medulla and is grossly in excess of the metabolic needs of the kidneys. It is largely unrelated to arterial pressure and is able to alter renal vascular resistance to maintain renal blood flow at a fairly constant level. Renal blood flow is reduced by fear and emotional stress due to constriction of renal blood vessels but is unchanged by noradrenaline administration.

STATISTICS AND EPIDEMIOLOGY

The answers and teaching notes to this section start on page 95.

161. In statistical analysis

- ☐ A the mean is always less than the mode
- ☐ B there is the same number of observations greater than and less than the median value
- ☐ C the standard deviation is always greater than the standard error of the mean
- ☐ D the standard deviation is independent of the total number of observations
- ☐ E the median value always lies at the midpoint of the range

162. In statistical analysis

- ☐ A Student's t-test is the standard method of comparing the observed and expected frequencies of an event
- ☐ B the Chi-squared test is the standard method for comparing the size of variances
- ☐ C the variance is the square root of the standard deviation (SD)
- ☐ D the normal range contains the central 90% of the observations in a population
- ☐ E the confidence interval is the interval containing the unknown true value of the parameter with a known probability

163. The standard deviation

- ☐ A is a test of significance
- ☐ B gives an indication of the scatter of the observations
- ☐ C can only apply to a normal distribution
- ☐ D is calculated from the mean and the number of observations
- ☐ E is the same as the median

164. Survival data

☐ A contain information about the time taken for individuals to reach a defined end-point
☐ B are said to be censored when there is incomplete observation of the 'failure' time (where failure represents death)
☐ C comparing two groups are analysed by actuarial survival curves
☐ D comparing two groups is not appropriate when data are sensored
☐ E may be analysed by the Kaplan-Meier analysis

165. Cancer of the cervix uteri

☐ A has a peak age incidence at age 35 to 40 years
☐ B accounts for approximately 1000 deaths annually in the UK
☐ C is more common in smokers
☐ D is more commonly found in those from lower socio-economic groups
☐ E in this country is falling in incidence in those under 40 years of age

166. In the normal distribution

☐ A the mean and mode are equal
☐ B the median is one standard deviation below the mean
☐ C 99.7% of the population lies within two standard deviations of the mean
☐ D the standard error of the mean is the variance divided by the square root of the number of observations
☐ E the distribution is unimodal

167. The definition of

☐ A the prevalence of a disease is the number of patients who develop the disease in a given period of time
☐ B the sensitivity of a test is the probability of the test being positive in patients with the condition
☐ C the specificity of a test is the probability of having the condition if the test is positive
☐ D neonatal death is death within 28 days of birth
☐ E infant mortality rate is the number of infants dying during the first year per 1000 live births

ANSWERS AND TEACHING NOTES :
STATISTICS AND EPIDEMIOLOGY

161. B C

The mean or the average (strictly the arithmetic mean) is the sum of all the observations divided by the number of observations. The mode is the most commonly occurring value in a set of values, therefore the mean is not always less than the mode. The median is the middle observation in a set of observations arranged in order of magnitude.

The standard deviation is a measure of the spread of observations and should be reported with the estimated mean when the aim is to describe the distribution of the data. The standard error of the mean relates to the precision of the estimated mean and therefore is less than the standard deviation.

162. E

The Student's t-test compares the difference between two means. The chi-squared test compares the observed and expected frequencies of an event. The variance is the square of the SD. The normal range contains the central 95% of the observations in a population.

163. B C D

The standard deviation is the positive square root of the variance and is an indicator of dispersion (scatter) of observations. It applies to the normal distribution. The median is the middle observation in a set of observations arranged in order of magnitude.

164. A B D E

Actuarial survival curves are concerned with the distribution of survival times in a single group and can be used when not all subjects in the study have reached the defined end-point (often five years when calculating survival in cancer patients). The Kaplan-Meier analysis is based on precise survival times.

165. C D

Cancer of the cervix has a peak age incidence at about 50 years of age. It is more common in those from so-called lower socio-economic groups and accounts for approximately 2000 deaths annually. This is despite the cervical smear screening programme. It is actually increasing in younger women (arbitrarily taken as 40 years or less).

166. A E

The mode is the most commonly occurring value in a set of values and therefore in a normal distribution the mode and mean are equal. The median is the middle observation in a set of observations arranged in order of magnitude. In a normal distribution, approximately 95% are contained in the interval which spans the mean by two standard deviations on either side of it. The variance is the arithmetic mean of the squared deviations. The standard error of the mean is the *standard deviation* divided by the square root of the number of observations.

167. B D E

The prevalence of a disease is the number of patients in a defined population who have the disease at the time of the study. The incidence of a disease refers to the number developing the disease in a given period of time. A test with a 50% sensitivity, for example, will mean that only 50% of patients with the disease will have a positive result. If the specificity of a test is less than 100% it means that there will be false-positive results; it is the probability of a negative test given the absence of the condition.

PRACTICE EXAMS

INSTRUCTIONS

In order to help MRCOG Part 1 candidates revise for this difficult examination we have tried to follow as closely as possible the content and format of the official examination. Each question has an answer and teaching explanation which should provide a good basis for successful revision.

We suggest that you work on each set of 60 multiple choice questions as though it was a real MRCOG examination. In other words time yourself to spend no more than 2 hours on each practice exam and do not obtain help from books, notes or persons while working on each test. Plan to take each practice exam at a time when you will be undisturbed for a minimum of 2 hours. Choose a well lit location free from distractions, keep your desk clear of other books or papers, have a clock or watch clearly visible with a rubber and 2 well sharpened grade B pencils to hand.

As you work through each question in this book be sure to mark a tick or cross (True or False) in the box against each A... B... C... D... E... answer option. If you do not know the answer then leave the answer space blank. Thus when you have completed the paper you can mark your own answers with the help of the answers and explanations given at the end of the book. Do not be tempted to look at the questions before sitting down to take each test as this will not then represent a mock exam.

When you have finished an exam be sure to go back over your answers until the 2 hours is over. When your time is up you can then mark your answers and study the teaching explanations carefully so as to learn from your mistakes. Give yourself + 1 for every correct answer, -1 for every incorrect answer and 0 for an unanswered question. Put a mark clearly on the book wherever you put a wrong answer and this will help you with your final revision as the official exam grows near.

Good luck with your revision.

PRACTICE EXAM 1

60 Questions : time allowed 2 hours.
Indicate your answers with a tick or cross (True or False) in the box provided.

1. **The uterine cervix**

   ☐ A undergoes cyclical changes during the menstrual cycle
   ☐ B sheds its lining at menstruation
   ☐ C has a lining of columnar epithelium in its canal
   ☐ D may have glands opening onto its vaginal surface
   ☐ E has peritoneum on the posterior surface of its supravaginal part

2. **The rectum**

   ☐ A is covered anteriorly by peritoneum along its whole length
   ☐ B has no taeniae coli
   ☐ C has appendices epiploicae
   ☐ D has a blood supply from the terminal branches of the superior mesenteric artery
   ☐ E has permanent transverse folds consisting of mucous membrane and circular smooth muscle

3. **The following statements relating to the small intestine are correct:**

   ☐ A the small intestine becomes narrower throughout its course
   ☐ B circular folds (valves of Kerckring) are more frequent in the ileum than in the jejunum
   ☐ C villi are shorter in the jejunum than in the ileum
   ☐ D Brunner's glands are most frequent in the jejunum
   ☐ E Paneth cells are found only in the bases of the crypts of Lieberkühn

4. **In the kidney**

   ☐ A the columns of Bertini contain cortical tissue
   ☐ B all nephrons have equally long loops of Henle
   ☐ C the afferent arteriole at the glomerulus has a thicker muscular wall than the efferent arteriole
   ☐ D the macula densa arises from the wall of the proximal convoluted tubule
   ☐ E the renal pelvis contains smooth muscle fibres

5. **The round ligament**

☐ A is over 25 cm long
☐ B runs posterior to the obturator artery
☐ C is embryologically related to the ovarian ligament
☐ D passes lateral to the inferior epigastric artery
☐ E contains striated muscle fibres

6. **The following statements relating to the adrenal glands are correct:**

☐ A the average weight of the normal adrenal gland in the adult is one gram
☐ B each gland is drained by three separate veins
☐ C the medulla is endodermal in origin
☐ D the zona reticularis of the cortex lies next to the medulla
☐ E aldosterone is produced by cells of the zona glomerulosa of the cortex

7. **The following are primary branches of the coeliac artery:**

☐ A left gastric artery
☐ B right gastro-epiploic artery
☐ C gastro-duodenal artery
☐ D hepatic artery
☐ E splenic artery

8. **The following are synovial joints:**

☐ A symphysis pubis
☐ B sacro-iliac
☐ C sacro-coccygeal
☐ D lumbo-sacral
☐ E patello-femoral

9. **Prolactin**

☐ A is structurally related to human placental lactogen (HPL)
☐ B is secreted by basophil cells of the anterior pituitary
☐ C is increased in the circulation after section of the pituitary stalk
☐ D is secreted in reduced amounts in patients taking chlorpromazine
☐ E can only be measured by bioassay

10. **The following are therapeutically radiosensitive human genital tract tumours:**

☐ A squamous cell carcinoma of cervix
☐ B adenocarcinoma of cervix
☐ C carcinoma of vulva
☐ D dysgerminoma
☐ E adenocarcinoma of endometrium

11. **Hypokalaemia may lead to**

☐ A paralytic ileus
☐ B mental confusion
☐ C increased sensitivity of the renal tubules to antidiuretic hormone (ADH)
☐ D aciduria
☐ E elevation of the ST segment on the electrocardiogram

12. **Spermatozoa**

☐ A contain 23 chromosomes
☐ B are produced at a faster rate when testicular temperature is raised
☐ C require testosterone for normal development
☐ D require follicle-stimulating hormone (FSH) for normal development
☐ E are produced from spermatogonia in approximately 20 days

13. During normal pregnancy

- [ ] A blood cholesterol levels decrease
- [ ] B blood free fatty acids increase
- [ ] C blood vitamin C levels increase
- [ ] D ketones appear more rapidly during starvation
- [ ] E iodine uptake by the thyroid gland increases

14. In a baby with ambiguous genitalia

- [ ] A the presence of unilateral Mullerian structures implies testicular tissue on the contralateral wall
- [ ] B the uterus will be absent if excess adrenal androgens were the cause (congenital adrenal hyperplasia)
- [ ] C the uterus will be absent in 5 alpha-reductase deficiency
- [ ] D fusion of the labioscrotal folds indicates a male chromosome constitution
- [ ] E a normal 46XX karyotype strongly suggests excess androgens

15. Acquired immune deficiency syndrome (AIDS)

- [ ] A is caused by a DNA virus
- [ ] B is due to a virus binding to CD4 molecule on T-cells
- [ ] C may be transmitted by artificial insemination
- [ ] D in its clinical form is likely to lead to death within 5 years
- [ ] E in the pregnant woman is likely to result in a 30% chance of transmission to the fetus

16. In the autonomic nervous system

- [ ] A acetylcholine is the mediator at all synapses between pre- and post-ganglionic nerves
- [ ] B pseudocholinesterase is localised at nerve endings
- [ ] C strychnine blocks the action of inhibitory interneurones in the spinal cord
- [ ] D adrenaline is the mediator of activity at most post-ganglionic sympathetic nerve endings
- [ ] E dopaminergic neurones are present in sympathetic ganglia

17. **Human chorionic gonadotrophin (HCG)**

- [ ] A is a glycoprotein
- [ ] B is secreted by the trophoblast prior to implantation
- [ ] C has a beta subunit similar to follicle stimulating hormone (FSH)
- [ ] D reaches a peak level at 20 weeks' gestation
- [ ] E is involved in the induction of fetal testosterone secretion

18. **The following drugs have been shown to be teratogenic to the human fetus:**

- [ ] A thiazide diuretics
- [ ] B tetracyclines
- [ ] C metronidazole
- [ ] D heparin
- [ ] E azothioprine

19. **Folic acid**

- [ ] A deficiency leads to megaloblastic anaemia
- [ ] B is water soluble
- [ ] C does not require gastric intrinsic factor for its absorption
- [ ] D is found only in animal foods
- [ ] E is necessary for nucleic acid synthesis

20. **Gastrin**

- [ ] A is an enzyme produced in the stomach
- [ ] B stimulates the production of acid by the stomach
- [ ] C is produced in increased amounts in response to protein meals
- [ ] D is secreted by the neck cells of the gastric glands
- [ ] E effects are mimicked by histamine

21. **During respiration**

☐ A the amount of air that moves into the lungs with each respiration is the tidal volume

☐ B the volume inspired with a maximal inspiratory effort in excess of the tidal volume is the total lung volume

☐ C the respiratory dead space is that space occupied by gas that does not exchange with blood in the pulmonary vessels

☐ D the functional capacity is reduced in pregnancy

☐ E the vital capacity is the greatest amount of air that can be expired after a passive expiration

22. **The following genetic conditions are sex-linked:**

☐ A the 'hairy pinna' trait

☐ B cleft palate

☐ C Hurler's syndrome (type 1 mucopolysaccaridosis)

☐ D achondroplasia

☐ E congenital ichthyosis

23. **Diazoxide**

☐ A is related chemically to the thiazide diuretics

☐ B leads to vasodilatation

☐ C does not bind appreciably to plasma proteins

☐ D leads to sodium and water retention

☐ E depresses insulin secretion from the beta cells of the pancreatic islets

24. **Labetolol**

☐ A is an alpha-blocking drug

☐ B is a beta-blocking drug

☐ C use may lead to cold extremities

☐ D is safe in pregnancy

☐ E causes more postural hypotension than propranolol

25. The obturator nerve

☐ A has a root value of L3, 4, 5
☐ B gives an articular branch to the hip joint
☐ C supplies adductor magnus
☐ D gives an articular branch to the knee joint
☐ E supplies the gracilis muscle

26. The karyotype 47 XXY is associated with

☐ A mongolism
☐ B a single Barr body
☐ C the presence of an ovotestis
☐ D gynaecomastia
☐ E an increased incidence of mental retardation

27. In mammalian cell division

☐ A cytokinesis is the process by which two daughter cells form at the end of telophase
☐ B chromosomes migrate to separate sides of the cell in metaphase
☐ C prophase takes 2 to 3 hours
☐ D the number of chromosomes is constant in any given species
☐ E most cancer cells have 46 chromosomes

28. Arginine vasopressin

☐ A is produced by cells of the anterior pituitary gland
☐ B increases the permeability of the collecting ducts of the kidney to water
☐ C is released in response to alcohol consumption
☐ D is produced in excess in diabetes insipidus
☐ E is a decapeptide

29. The standard deviation

- ☐ A is a test of significance
- ☐ B is a measure of the scatter of observations about their mean
- ☐ C is only meaningful if the observations have a normal distribution
- ☐ D is calculated from the mean and number of observations alone
- ☐ E is the same as a centile

30. Amniotic fluid

- ☐ A volume is related to gestational age
- ☐ B has no contributions from the fetal kidneys
- ☐ C alphafetoprotein level increases with gestation in the second trimester of pregnancy
- ☐ D contains no creatinine
- ☐ E osmolality increases to term

31. Cytoplasmic messenger RNA

- ☐ A is translated from DNA
- ☐ B is larger than heterogeneous RNA
- ☐ C contains uracil in place of thymidine
- ☐ D is manufactured in the 1-cell embryo
- ☐ E contains codons for amino acids consisting of four bases

32. During implantation

- ☐ A the blastocyst cavity is obliterated and replaced by the yolk sac
- ☐ B the secondary yolk sac is formed in the extra-embryonic mesenchyme
- ☐ C the primitive streak develops 7 days after fertilization
- ☐ D syncytiotrophoblast forms
- ☐ E monozygotic twinning may occur

33. *Candida albicans*

- [ ] A is a bacterium
- [ ] B grows readily in Sabouraud's medium
- [ ] C has an increased incidence in diabetes mellitus
- [ ] D is characterised by a flagellum
- [ ] E is treated by nystatin

34. Vitamin K

- [ ] A is required for the synthesis of prothrombin
- [ ] B is water soluble
- [ ] C deficiency may contribute to haemorrhagic disease of the newborn
- [ ] D deficiency may result from the use of broad spectrum antibiotics
- [ ] E may be deficient in the diet of certain food fadists

35. In the development of the female genital tract

- [ ] A the Mullerian ducts fuse at their lower end to form the uterus and cervix
- [ ] B the Fallopian tubes are formed from the Wolffian ducts
- [ ] C the urogenital sinus receives the mesonephric ducts
- [ ] D the lower part of the vagina is derived from the sino-vaginal bulbs
- [ ] E the urogenital sinus is continuous with the allantois

36. In the blood in pregnancy

- [ ] A the total red cell mass increases during the second trimester
- [ ] B the plasma volume is expanded more in the cases of pregnancy-induced hypertension than normal of the same gestation
- [ ] C a neutrophil leucocytosis is characteristic
- [ ] D the mean corpuscular haemoglobin concentration increases in folate deficiency
- [ ] E a mean red cell volume of 75 fl at 16 weeks' gestation is of no clinical significance

37. Tuberculosis

- ☐ A of the genital tract commonly originates in the lungs
- ☐ B can cause sterility
- ☐ C does not occur in pregnant women
- ☐ D is satisfactorily treated by a 3 month course of para-amino salicyclic acid
- ☐ E organisms resist decolorisation by 20% sulphuric acid after Ziehl Neelsen staining

38. Characteristics of malignant tumours include

- ☐ A a cell production rate greater than that of adjacent normal tissue
- ☐ B a tendency to metastasise
- ☐ C aneuploidy
- ☐ D sensitivity to irradiation
- ☐ E poor differentiation

39. The gonococcus

- ☐ A is a Gram-positive organism
- ☐ B grows well in anaerobic conditions
- ☐ C occasionally causes a disseminated infection
- ☐ D can cause bartholinitis
- ☐ E is always penicillin sensitive

40. The following drugs are teratogenic:

- ☐ A cyclophosphamide
- ☐ B penicillin
- ☐ C heparin
- ☐ D testosterone
- ☐ E sodium barbitone

41. Parathormone

- [ ] A is produced by the C-cells of the thyroid gland
- [ ] B decreases urinary excretion of calcium
- [ ] C blood level increases when serum calcium falls
- [ ] D depresses activity of the anterior pituitary
- [ ] E is independent of magnesium levels

42. Exfoliative cytology

- [ ] A involves the study of wax-embedded pieces of tissue
- [ ] B is performed on cells aspirated through a fine needle
- [ ] C is used to screen for carcinoma of the uterine cervix
- [ ] D may be used to diagnose carcinoma of the ovary
- [ ] E is often used in the diagnosis of breast lesions

43. The following diseases are caused by bacteria:

- [ ] A toxic shock syndrome
- [ ] B syphilis
- [ ] C infectious mononucleosis
- [ ] D rubella
- [ ] E rabies

44. Granulation tissue

- [ ] A contains fibroblasts
- [ ] B always contains granulomas
- [ ] C often occurs after short-lived injury to the liver
- [ ] D contains thin-walled capillaries
- [ ] E actively contracts

45. Following the loss of one litre of blood in a 70 kg individual there is

- [ ] A a decreased concentration of plasma proteins
- [ ] B a decreased capillary hydrostatic pressure
- [ ] C sodium retention
- [ ] D a decreased secretion of vasopressin
- [ ] E an increased concentration in plasma of vasopressin

46. In the process of human lactation

☐ A colostrum is rich in protein
☐ B prolactin secretion increases
☐ C progesterone concentrations fall
☐ D oxytocin is essential for milk ejection
☐ E amenorrhoea is common

47. Thyroxine

☐ A formation requires the amino acid tyrosine
☐ B is less than 80% bound to plasma proteins
☐ C is essential for skeletal development
☐ D increases oxygen consumption in the brain
☐ E leads to an increased serum cholesterol level when present in excess in the circulation

48. The mode of action of the following cytotoxic agents is:

☐ A vinblastine-antimetabolite
☐ B tamoxifen-oestrogen agonist
☐ C 5-fluorouracil-alkylating agent
☐ D adriamycin-antibiotic
☐ E cyclophosphamide-alkylating agent

49. The following may be constituents of emboli:

☐ A clot
☐ B tumour
☐ C fat
☐ D calculi
☐ E gas

50. Normal micturition

☐ A depends on the integrity of a sacral spinal reflex arc
☐ B is prevented by sectioning the sensory nerves supplying the bladder
☐ C may occur with spinal transection in the thoracic region
☐ D follows activation of the sympathetic nerves to the bladder
☐ E is under voluntary control in healthy young adults

51. The right ovary

- ☐ A receives its blood supply from the aorta
- ☐ B is attached to the anterior leaf of the broad ligament
- ☐ C is attached to the suspensory ligament of the ovary at its lateral pole
- ☐ D is covered by peritoneum in the adult
- ☐ E has veins which drain to the inferior vena cava

52. The Fallopian tube

- ☐ A is lined by ciliated columnar epithelium
- ☐ B is attached by the fimbria to the lateral pole of the ovary
- ☐ C undergoes cyclical changes during the menstrual cycle
- ☐ D arises from the paramesonephric duct
- ☐ E is narrower at its lateral than medial end

53. The middle third of the vagina

- ☐ A has a stratified squamous keratinising epithelium
- ☐ B is related to the pouch of Douglas posteriorly
- ☐ C receives part of its blood supply from the inferior vesical arteries
- ☐ D is mesodermal in origin
- ☐ E is derived from the mesonephric duct

54. The female breast

- ☐ A is developmentally a collection of modified sweat glands
- ☐ B is drained mainly by lymphatics going direct to the supraclavicular nodes
- ☐ C develops a large amount of secretory tissue at puberty
- ☐ D has a separate duct for each lobe, opening onto the nipple
- ☐ E never extends laterally over serratus anterior

55. **Human leucocyte antigens (HLA) are**

☐ A genetically determined by the major histocompatability complex (MHC)
☐ B present only on leucocytes
☐ C usually two in number on human leucocytes
☐ D involved in transplantation immunity
☐ E glycoproteins

56. **Clinical trials**

☐ A are usually randomised and controlled
☐ B compare the efficacy of different medical treatments when they are administered to patients
☐ C must not use historical controls if they are to be statistically valid
☐ D must involve the study of at least 1000 subjects (patients)
☐ E should always be double-blind

57. **The femoral canal**

☐ A is medial to the femoral vein at its proximal end
☐ B contains the femoral branch of the genito-femoral nerve
☐ C has the femoral ring at its lower end
☐ D contains lymph vessels
☐ E is posterior to the inguinal ligament at its proximal end

58. **The typical female bony pelvis**

☐ A has a transverse diameter at the inlet greater than the antero-posterior diameter
☐ B has an obstetric conjugate of 11-12 cm
☐ C is funnel-shaped
☐ D has an obtuse greater sciatic notch
☐ E has a subpubic angle greater than 90 degrees

59. The tricarboxylic cycle (Krebs cycle)

- ☐ A is a source of adenosine triphosphate (ATP)
- ☐ B has a purely catabolic function
- ☐ C converts metabolic energy into chemical energy
- ☐ D provides for the complete combustion of fatty acids
- ☐ E requires co-enzyme for its continued operation

60. Vitamin B12

- ☐ A requires intrinsic factor for absorption
- ☐ B is water soluble
- ☐ C deficiency can be treated by oral supplementation
- ☐ D is only obtained from animal sources in the diet
- ☐ E is destroyed by cooking

Go over your answers until the 2 hours is up.
The correct answers and teaching notes are on page 129 onwards.

PRACTICE EXAM 2

60 Questions : time allowed 2 hours.
Indicate your answers with a tick or cross (True or False) in the box provided.

1. **Adequate sperm transport through the cervix is related to**

   ☐ A changes in the cervical mucus at ovulation
   ☐ B anaerobic fructolysis within the semen
   ☐ C suction of semen into the uterus at coitus
   ☐ D low pH within the cervical mucus
   ☐ E uterine anterversion

2. **Prostaglandins**

   ☐ A are polypeptides found in prostatic fluid
   ☐ B induce rhythmic uterine contractions in a similar way to oxytocin
   ☐ C cause constipation in man
   ☐ D formation is inhibited by aspirin
   ☐ E PgF2alpha may cause bronchoconstriction

3. **The following factors positively influence high birth weight:**

   ☐ A maternal growth hormone
   ☐ B prolonged pregnancy (294 days)
   ☐ C fetal hyperinsulinaemia
   ☐ D primiparity
   ☐ E social class

4. **Adenocarcinoma in situ (ACIS) of the cervix**

   ☐ A is more common than squamous carcinoma in situ (cervical intraepithial neoplasia) of the cervix
   ☐ B may develop into invasive adenocarcinoma
   ☐ C has a positive association with use of the oral contraceptive pill
   ☐ D is more easily detected by cervical cytology than its squamous counterpart
   ☐ E is increasing in detected incidence

5. **Endometrial hyperplasia**

☐ A is associated with obesity
☐ B of the simple type, is associated with an increased risk of endometrial adenocarcinoma
☐ C is associated with unopposed oestrogenic stimulation
☐ D may be diagnosed clinically
☐ E is more common in post- than in pre-menopausal women

6. **Uterine fibroids (leiomyomas)**

☐ A are the commonest tumours of the female genital tract
☐ B are associated with high parity
☐ C may cause subfertility
☐ D may cause abnormal uterine bleeding
☐ E may measure up to 200 mm in diameter

7. **Gynaecomastia**

☐ A occurs most frequently in the third decade of life
☐ B has histological appearances which include stromal oedema and epithelial proliferation
☐ C is associated with endocrine disturbance
☐ D has been associated with treated prostatic carcinoma
☐ E may occur with chlorpromazine administration

8. **The human Fallopian tube**

☐ A contains only ciliated cells
☐ B has four muscular layers
☐ C usually contains the fertilised ovum for six days
☐ D epithelium has cyclic variation
☐ E isthmo-ampullary junction is not clearly demarcated

9. **In the labia majora**

☐ A the blood supply is derived from the internal and external pudendal arteries

☐ B a persistent processus vaginalis may be present

☐ C venous drainage does not connect with the dorsal veins of the clitoris

☐ D Meissner corpuscles are present

☐ E lymphatic systems are separate on each side

10. **The ureter**

☐ A is lined with columnar epithelium

☐ B has four muscle layers

☐ C passes down on the psoas muscle and crosses the bifurcation of the common iliac artery

☐ D derives its blood supply for the upper portion from the vesical artery

☐ E is of mesodermal origin

11. **The bladder**

☐ A receives its parasympathetic nerve supply from S2, S3, S4

☐ B is lined with transitional epithelium

☐ C has a mobile trigone

☐ D muscle and mucosal walls are pierced obliquely by the ureters

☐ E epithelium is ectodermal in origin

12. **The following statements relating to the ischial spines are correct:**

☐ A they lie between the greater and lesser sciatic notches

☐ B they mark the beginning of the forward curve of the birth canal

☐ C they are of particular prominence in the normal female pelvis

☐ D when the widest diameter of the fetal skull is at the level of the spines, the head is not yet engaged

☐ E the internal pudendal nerve lies in close relationship to the spines

13. **The right ovary**

☐ A has a blood supply from the abdominal aorta
☐ B is attached to the anterior (inferior) layer of the broad ligament
☐ C has the ovarian ligament attached to its medial pole
☐ D is covered by peritoneum in the adult
☐ E is drained by veins which go to the superior vena cava

14. **The uterine artery**

☐ A is a branch of the internal iliac artery
☐ B passes below the ureter in the broad ligament
☐ C does not supply the cervix
☐ D eventually forms an anastomosis with the tubal branch of the ovarian artery
☐ E directly supplies the round ligament

15. **Branches of the internal iliac artery include**

☐ A internal pudendal
☐ B obturator
☐ C superior gluteal
☐ D middle rectal
☐ E ovarian

16. **The pudendal nerve**

☐ A arises from sacral nerves S2, S3, S4
☐ B lies lateral to the pudendal vessels
☐ C lies medial to the ischial spine
☐ D passes through the greater sciatic foramen
☐ E terminates as the perineal nerve

17. **The femoral nerve**

☐ A is derived from the posterior division of lumbar nerves 2, 3 and 4
☐ B lies in the iliac fossa between psoas and iliacus muscles
☐ C lies medial to the femoral artery
☐ D lies lateral to the femoral vein
☐ E enters the thigh inside the femoral sheath

18. A woman whose blood group is O rhesus-negative

- ☐ A has the commonest blood type
- ☐ B has no antibodies to the ABO system in her blood
- ☐ C carries A and B antigens on the red cells
- ☐ D should receive only O rhesus-negative blood if transfusion is required
- ☐ E should always receive anti-D immunoglobulin following childbirth

19. The following are steroid hormones:

- ☐ A cortisol
- ☐ B vitamin D
- ☐ C aldosterone
- ☐ D corticotrophin-releasing factor
- ☐ E adrenocorticotrophin

20. Rhesus isoimmunisation

- ☐ A is less common in ABO incompatible pregnancies
- ☐ B occurs in only 5% of exposed Rh -ve mothers
- ☐ C is usually due to anti-E
- ☐ D is due to cell bound antibodies
- ☐ E is determined by antigens limited to the red cell surface

21. Vitamin B12 (cyanocobalamin)

- ☐ A absorption occurs from the large intestine
- ☐ B occurs in certain plant products
- ☐ C is shorter-lasting than hydroxocobalamin
- ☐ D and folic acid are antagonistic with regard to the formation of myelin
- ☐ E deficiency leads to pernicious anaemia

22. Glucose transfer across the placenta

☐ A is energy dependent
☐ B is much slower at high concentrations (more than 22 mol/l)
☐ C is more rapid than fructose transfer
☐ D is not dependent on a concentration gradient
☐ E is glucagon dependent

23. Renin

☐ A has a molecular weight of 65,000
☐ B is only produced in the kidney
☐ C is released when there is a rise in blood pressure
☐ D is released by decreased blood sodium concentration
☐ E falls in amount with a rise in plasma potassium

24. In adult human blood

☐ A the monocyte is the largest of the circulating white cells
☐ B the mature lymphocyte has a basophilic cytoplasm
☐ C 10% of the polymorphonuclear leucocytes in female subjects show a nuclear appendage
☐ D packed cell volume is less in women than in men
☐ E eosinophils constitute between 10 and 20% of the white cell count under normal conditions

25. Human chorionic gonadotrophin (HCG)

☐ A has the biological properties of LH (luteinising hormone)
☐ B can transform a normal cyclic corpus luteum into a pseudopregnant corpus luteum
☐ C is responsible for the onset of parturition
☐ D is detectable in maternal serum before implantation of the ovum
☐ E is significantly elevated in pre-eclampsia

26. In the human fetus

- ☐ A the adrenal cortex contains a distinct cellular zone that disappears after birth
- ☐ B human growth hormone reaches its peak at birth
- ☐ C the pancreas responds to high levels of glucose
- ☐ D noradrenaline is produced solely by the adrenal medulla
- ☐ E the pituitary contains a pars intermedia

27. Oxytocin is

- ☐ A a lipid hormone
- ☐ B synthesised in the anterior hypothalamic nuclei
- ☐ C released directly into the circulation from its site of production
- ☐ D an anti-diuretic
- ☐ E relatively inactive in early pregnancy

28. In progesterone production and metabolism

- ☐ A only 10% of circulating hormone is free
- ☐ B the main source of the hormone in human pregnancy is the corpus luteum
- ☐ C cholesterol is a precursor
- ☐ D liver is the main site of degradation
- ☐ E the hormone causes increased excitability of the myometrium

29. Prostaglandin E2

- ☐ A is a uterine smooth muscle stimulant
- ☐ B is a protein hormone
- ☐ C production is inhibited by indomethacin
- ☐ D is released by platelets during blood coagulation
- ☐ E is an antidiuretic

30. Interferons

- ☐ A are produced by virus-infected cells
- ☐ B are glyoproteins
- ☐ C are produced by recombinant RNA technology
- ☐ D may exert direct inhibitory effects on tumour cell growth
- ☐ E may produce a severe influenza-like syndrome

31. *Chlamydia trachomatis*

- ☐ A does not have a cell wall
- ☐ B is an obligatory intracellular parasite
- ☐ C can be easily detected by means of light microscopy
- ☐ D is often carried asymptomatically on the female cervix
- ☐ E is a recognised cause of neonatal pneumonia

32. Genital warts

- ☐ A are the commonest viral sexually transmitted disease
- ☐ B are seen usually in patients over the age of 40
- ☐ C can be treated by means of salicylic acid
- ☐ D generally improve during pregnancy
- ☐ E may be associated with cervical cytological abnormalities

33. In human immunodeficiency virus (HIV)

- ☐ A on a global scale the main mode of transmission is by sexual intercourse between men
- ☐ B HIV II is found mainly in natives of the USA
- ☐ C the acute infection is usually symptomatic
- ☐ D approximately 90% of HIV-infected pregnant females will transmit the virus to their babies
- ☐ E oral hairy leukoplakia is unique to HIV infection

34. Histamine

- ☐ A causes local vasoconstriction
- ☐ B is found in mast cell granules
- ☐ C increases vascular permeability
- ☐ D is partially responsible for the triple response
- ☐ E stimulates gastric secretion

35. In the development of the human gonads and ducts

- ☐ A differentiation occurs later in the female
- ☐ B the caudal part of the female Mullerian duct degenerates to form Gartner's duct
- ☐ C Sertoli cells are derivatives of primordial sex cells
- ☐ D the Mullerian duct is an invagination of ectodermal tissue
- ☐ E the Mullerian tubercle is the site of the future hymen

36. The following statements concerning autosomal recessive disorders are correct:

- ☐ A both sexes are affected
- ☐ B the disorder is inherited from only one parent
- ☐ C the sibling of an affected child has a one in four chance of being affected
- ☐ D the rarer a recessive disease the greater the frequency of consanguinity among parents of an affected child
- ☐ E a grandparent of an affected child may be affected

37. The standard deviation of a group of observations

- ☐ A is the square of the variance of the group
- ☐ B is a measure of the scatter of observations around the mean
- ☐ C has a normal Gaussian distribution
- ☐ D may be used as a basis of the calculation of chi-squared
- ☐ E either side of the mean encompasses 75% of the observations

38. In the fetus

- ☐ A the umbilical arteries carry oxygenated blood
- ☐ B the ductus venosus short circuits the capillaries of the liver
- ☐ C the right atrium contains a mixture of oxygenated and venous blood
- ☐ D the foramen ovale connects the ventricles of the heart
- ☐ E the ductus arteriosus joins the aorta proximal to the aortic arch

39. The adult human haemoglobin A

- ☐ A has a molecular weight of 20,000
- ☐ B has a globulin portion containing predominantly alpha and gamma chains
- ☐ C has a higher affinity for oxygen than fetal haemoglobin (HgbF)
- ☐ D is produced at a rate of 6 g per day in normal conditions
- ☐ E contains haem groups which are porphyrin-only structures

40. Ergometrine

- ☐ A takes 2.5 mins to cause uterine contraction in the post-partum woman when given intramuscularly
- ☐ B has anti-emetic properties
- ☐ C may cause tachycardia
- ☐ D should be used only with caution in pre-eclamptic patients
- ☐ E is more effective towards term than in early pregnancy

41. During the process of fertilisation and implantation

- ☐ A fertilisation occurs in the outer third of the Fallopian tube
- ☐ B the haploid number of chromosomes results
- ☐ C the morula is enclosed by trophoblast
- ☐ D the morula actively moves along the oviduct
- ☐ E human chorionic gonadotrophin (HCG) is produced by the preimplantation embryo

42. Amniotic fluid

- [ ] A has an acid pH
- [ ] B increases in volume after the 37th week
- [ ] C organic constituents are mainly lipid
- [ ] D decreases in volume with intrauterine growth retardation
- [ ] E protein content decreases after the 26th week

43. Calcium absorption is

- [ ] A increased in diets containing high protein
- [ ] B decreased in coeliac disease
- [ ] C increased in high phosphate diets
- [ ] D decreased by calcitonin
- [ ] E decreased in chronic pancreatitis

44. During the normal menstrual cycle in the human

- [ ] A basal vacuolation is the earliest histological evidence of ovulation
- [ ] B gland mitosis occurs in the menstruating endometrium
- [ ] C endometrial regeneration occurs from the zona pellucida
- [ ] D the secretory or postovulatory changes in the endometrium are brought about by oestrogen action
- [ ] E spiral arterial changes initiate endometrial menstrual breakdown

45. As used in statistics, the median of a series of observations is the

- [ ] A sum total of values divided by the number of observations
- [ ] B centre value with the observations ranged in order from highest to lowest
- [ ] C value occurring most often
- [ ] D distance between the highest and lowest values
- [ ] E square root of the standard deviation

46. Streptococci

☐ A are all Gram-positive
☐ B are solely aerobic
☐ C are the main cause of infective endocarditis
☐ D are arranged in characteristic grape-like clusters in Gram-stained preparation
☐ E typically produce the enzyme coagulase

47. The maternal serum alpha-fetoprotein concentration in pregnancy may be elevated in association with the following fetal conditions:

☐ A intrauterine death
☐ B congenital heart disease
☐ C twins
☐ D congenital nephrosis
☐ E microcephaly

48. The following statements relating to thyroid function are correct:

☐ A TRH is a decapeptide
☐ B placental thyrotrophin is biochemically identical to pituitary TSH
☐ C the metabolic activity of T3 is about four times that of T4
☐ D 5% of the circulating T4 is free (not protein bound)
☐ E circulating TBG increases under the influence of oestrogens

49. Progesterone

☐ A is natriuretic
☐ B requires oestrogen priming before it can demonstrate activity on the sexual organs
☐ C is synthesised in the adrenal gland
☐ D decreases uterine muscle contractility
☐ E is produced by arrhenoblastomas

50. The following features are characteristic of malignant tumours:

☐ A the presence of metastatic growth
☐ B absence of mitotic figures
☐ C invasion of surrounding tissues
☐ D loss of differentiation
☐ E in the majority, a rapid rate of growth

51. In the healthy neonate

☐ A the onset of physiological jaundice is between the 6th and 8th day
☐ B the bowel is sterile at birth
☐ C urine is not normally passed until 24 hours after birth
☐ D the respiratory rate is in the region of 25-35 per minute
☐ E the ductus arteriosus closes functionally within an hour of birth

52. The phaeochromocytoma

☐ A is a tumour of adrenal medullary tissue
☐ B is benign in the majority of cases
☐ C has its maximum incidence after the menopause
☐ D can be associated with severe episodes of hypotension
☐ E is always found in the adrenal gland

53. The pituitary gland

☐ A lies superior to the sphenoid bone
☐ B is all ectodermal
☐ C has the optic chiasma anteriorly
☐ D is supplied from the internal carotid artery
☐ E lies inferior to the cavernous sinus

54. Pregnancy is associated with

☐ A an increase in cardiac output
☐ B a decrease in central venous pressure
☐ C an increase in peripheral resistance
☐ D an increase in pulse rate
☐ E a decrease in stroke volume

55. **Respiratory changes in pregnancy include**

☐ A increase in the total lung capacity
☐ B increase in the airways resistance
☐ C decreased subcostal angle
☐ D decrease in vital capacity
☐ E increase in the minute volume

56. **In genital herpes**

☐ A the causative virus is an RNA virus
☐ B the incubation period of a primary attack is usually about 3 or 4 weeks
☐ C a primary attack is most likely to affect both the vulva and the cervix in females
☐ D recurrent attacks are likely to occur more frequently with HSV type 1 than HSV type 2
☐ E zidovudine is a useful agent in the treatment of genital herpes

57. **Fibrinogen**

☐ A is synthesised in bone marrow
☐ B decreases in concentration during pregnancy
☐ C has a normal plasma concentration of 50-100 mg per 100 ml
☐ D is converted to fibrin by thrombin
☐ E synthesis is dependent on vitamin K

58. **The following statements are correct:**

☐ A the ordinary diet in Great Britain provides 10-11 mg of iron each day
☐ B all of the daily ingested iron is absorbed
☐ C ingested iron is absorbed in the ferric form
☐ D 15% of ingested iron is absorbed
☐ E absorbed iron combines with apoferritin in the intestinal calls to form ferritin

59. Aldosterone causes

☐ A   a fall in urinary sodium excretion
☐ B   weight gain
☐ C   a fall in serum chloride levels
☐ D   increased extracellular fluid volume
☐ E   increased potassium excretion

60. In fat absorption and metabolism

☐ A   dietary fat is absorbed in the stomach
☐ B   dietary fat is absorbed in the form of chylomicrons
☐ C   the rate of cholesterol and myelin lipid synthesis is high in the adult central nervous system
☐ D   fatty acids are a major source of oxidative energy
☐ E   linoleic acid is an essential fatty acid

Go over your answers until the 2 hours is up.
The correct answers and teaching notes are on page 148 onwards.

ANSWERS AND TEACHING NOTES

PRACTICE EXAM 1

1. **A C D E**
   The cervix undergoes cyclical changes during the menstrual cycle; in particular, the amount of mucus secreted by the cervical glands alters. Columnar epithelium lines the canal and meets squamous epithelium at the squamo-columnar junction. This junction may lie in the canal or on the ectocervix (ectropion), therefore in the latter circumstance glands may open onto the vaginal surface. Only the lining of the endometrial cavity is shed at menstruation. Peritoneum is reflected onto the posterior aspect of the supravaginal cervix.

2. **B E**
   The upper part of the rectum is covered with peritoneum in front and at the sides; the middle part is covered in front only; the lower part lies below the level of the recto-vaginal pouch and therefore is devoid of peritoneal covering. Blood supply is from the inferior mesenteric artery through its rectal branches. Transverse folds project into the lumen consisting of mucous membrane and circular smooth muscle. Appendices epiploicae are not found in association with the rectum and taeniae coli are associated with the colon only.

3. **A E**
   The diameter of the jejunum is greater than that of the ileum. The valves become less frequent in the jejunum and disappear in the terminal ileum. There is a gradual decrease in villus size from pylorus to the ileo-caecal valve. Brunner's glands are found almost exclusively in the duodenum.

4. **A E**
   Juxtamedullary nephrons have much longer loops than outer cortical nephrons. The afferent arteriole is the thicker (and thus sensitive to angiotensin II). The junction between the ascending limb of the loop of Henle and the distal convoluted tubule is the site of the macula densa.

5. **C D**
   The round ligament is 10-12 cm long. It is a fibromuscular cord (smooth muscle) passing from the lateral angle of the uterus in the anterior layer of the broad ligament to the internal inguinal ring. Along with the ovarian ligament it is the pathway along which the female

gonad might have descended to the labium majus; it runs anteriorly to the obturator artery and passes lateral to the inferior epigastric artery.

6. **D E**
    The adrenal cortex and medulla have separate embryological origin, the cortex being derived from mesoderm and the medulla from the ectoderm. The average weight of the normal adult gland is 4 grams (range 2-6 grams). Each gland is supplied by three separate arteries but drained by a single vein. The zona reticularis lies next to the medulla and produces cortisol; aldosterone is predominantly synthesised by the cells of the zona glomerulosa.

7. **A D E**
    The primary branches of the coeliac axis are the hepatic artery, the splenic artery and the left gastric artery. The gastro-duodenal artery is a branch of the hepatic artery and therefore not a primary branch of the coeliac axis. The right gastro-epiploic artery is a branch of the gastro-duodenal artery.

8. **B E**
    A synovial joint consists of two ends of bone capped with hyaline cartilage and enclosed by an articular capsule. This consists of a fibrous capsule and a synovial membrane which produces the synovial fluid to keep the surfaces lubricated. The patello-femoral joint is a good example. The sacro-iliac joints are the articulations between the auricular surface of the sacrum and ilium on each side; they are synovium-lined and cartilage- covered joints. The sacro-coccygeal and the lumbo-sacral joints are intervertebral (symphysis) joints; their surfaces must be firmly bound to provide strength for their supporting function. Adjacent bodies are covered by a fibro-cartilagenous disc (annulus fibrosus); the centre of the disc is filled with fibro-cartilagenous pulp (nucleus pulposus), with no joint cavity. Each pubic bone is covered by a layer of hyaline cartilage and connected across the midline by a dense layer of fibro-cartilage.

9. **A C**
    Prolactin is a protein of molecular weight 20,000 and structurally is related to human placental lactogen. It is secreted by the acidophil cells of the anterior pituitary (along with growth hormone). A prolactin inhibitory factor is secreted by the hypothalamus and passes down the

hypothalamo-hypophyseal portal system to the anterior pituitary. Therefore section of the stalk reduces this inhibition and increases circulating prolactin levels. Chlorpromazine increases prolactin secretion probably by blocking receptors involved in the production of prolactin-inhibiting hormone; it is measured normally by a radioimmunoassay technique.

10. **A B D E**
Squamous cell carcinoma and adenocarcinoma of the cervix are equally sensitive to radiation. Dysgerminomas are very sensitive to radiation and chemotherapy. Carcinoma of the vulva is sensitive to high doses of radiation, but the effects on adjacent normal skin (ulceration, fibrosis) render the modality unsuitable for therapy except in advanced or recurrent disease. This part of the question illustrates the importance of studying every word of the stem where *therapeutically* is the key word.

11. **A B D**
Potassium is the principal cation in intracellular fluids. Deficiency, manifest by hypokalaemia, causes muscle weakness (both somatic and visceral), mental confusion and interferes with neuromuscular transmission. The latter is evidenced by ECG changes e.g. depression of the ST segment, flattening or inversion of T waves and prolongation of the PR interval. Hypokalaemia is associated with a reduced sensitivity of the renal tubules to ADH and the kidney therefore has a reduced concentrating ability, leading to frequency and polyuria. Since K^+ depletion and H^+ compete for Na^+ exchange in the proximal convoluted tubule in K depletion more H^+ will be lost in the urine and a metabolic alkalosis will result.

12. **A C D**
The male primitive germ cells, the spermatogonia, are diploid, as are the primary spermatocytes; thereafter a reduction division occurs such that the secondary spermatocytes, spermatids and mature spermatozoa are haploid with a chromosome complement of 23. FSH promotes spermatogenesis by a direct action on the seminiferous tubules; LH promotes secretion of androgens by the Leydig cells and these, testosterone in particular, are important also in stimulating spermatogenesis. The total sequence of spermatogenesis (the formation of spermatids) and spermiogenesis (the formation of

spermatozoa from spermatids) takes 65-75 days under normal circumstances. The process is however very sensitive to environmental changes particularly of temperature; the normal scrotal temperature is 1-2.5 °C lower than core temperature and even slight elevation will impair sperm production.

13. **B D E**
There is a general increase in plasma lipids during pregnancy. Levels of water-soluble vitamins decrease due to renal loss. As a result of oestrogen, HPL and other factors which promote fat breakdown and increase in acetyl co-enzyme A, ketones appear during starvation (for example in hyperemesis gravidarum). This ensures a supply of glucose to the fetus. Iodine uptake by the thyroid gland increases and urine loss is increased.

14. **A C E**
Mullerian activity is locally acting. The uterus will be present because there is no testicular tissue i.e. no Mullerian inhibitor. The external genitalia do not respond to normal androgen secretion by the testis but Mullerian inhibitor is produced in normal amounts. External genitalia respond passively to androgens and their appearance indicates severity not cause. In the absence of androgens a female external appearance will develop, whereas androgens produce a male phenotype irrespective of chromosome or gonadal sex.

15. **B C E**
HIV is an RNA virus which contains reverse transcriptase and gains entry to the T-cells via the CD4 molecules. Artificial insemination is a possible source of infection, making screening of donors imperative. Most patients with clinical AIDS will die within two years. The transmission rate of the virus across the placenta is approximately 30% and then clinical AIDS may be apparent within 4 months of birth.

16. **A C E**
Acetylcholine has been shown to be the transmitter substance released by pre-ganglionic fibres of both sympathetic and parasympathetic systems. Post-ganglionic fibres of the parasympathetic system also secrete acetylcholine, although with a few exceptions (e.g. sweat glands) sympathetic post-ganglionic fibres have noradrenaline as their transmitter. Interneurones of sympathetic ganglia secrete dopamine.

Acetylcholine is very quickly hydrolysed by a series of enzymes called cholinesterases which are present in high concentration at nerve terminals; pseudocholinesterase is present in plasma. Strychnine is a natural alkaloid, poisoning with which produces convulsions by abolishing the normal inhibitory effects of interneurones within the cord on spinal reflexes.

17. **A B E**
HCG is a glycoprotein composed of alpha and beta subunits. The alpha subunits are possessed also by thyroid-stimulating hormone, luteinising hormone (LH) and follicle-stimulating hormone (FSH). The beta subunit only shares characteristics with the beta subunit of LH. Secretion reaches a peak at 14 weeks' gestation and has fallen substantially by 20 weeks. There is now evidence of its involvement in the induction of fetal testosterone secretion.

18. **A B**
Thiazide diuretics may cause thrombocytopenia and bleeding disorders in the neonate. Heparin is of high molecular weight and does not cross the palcenta, unlike warfarin which may lead to bleeding disorders in the neonate if administered soon prior to delivery. Although an immunosuppressant and potentially toxic, experience of azothioprine in chronic auto-immune diseases and renal transplant recipients has as yet shown no adverse effect on the fetus. Metronidazole is safe in therapeutic dosage, but tetracycline produces staining of primary and secondary dentition.

19. **A B C E**
Folic acid is a water-soluble vitamin of the B group. It is widely disseminated in both plant and animal products although the main dietary source in man is green leafy vegetables. Unlike vitamin B12 which requires intrinsic factor for absorption it has no mediating absorptive mechanism and is assimilated throughout the small intestine. It is converted to the coenzyme tetrahydrofolinic acid which is important in the transfer of one-carbon units in purine synthesis; deficiency leads to a megaloblastic macrocytic anaemia.

20. **B C E**
Gastrin is not an enzyme but a polypeptide hormone secreted by cells in the pyloric antrum. This question emphasises the necessity to read

carefully all the words. One's attention is drawn to the word stomach and it would be easy to overlook the word enzyme. Protein, alcohol and caffeine all stimulate secretion, although carbohydrate and fats have a lesser effect. The major effect of gastrin is to stimulate acid secretion from the parietal cells in the glands of the body of the stomach (mucus neck cells also occur in the glands of the body which secrete mucus and intrinsic factor). Histamine is also a potent stimulant of gastric acid secretion and indeed it has been suggested that gastrin may act by causing histamine release from mast cells in the gastric mucosa.

21. **A C D**

The tidal volume is the amount of air inspired or expired with each respiration. The maximum volume that can be inspired beyond the tidal volume is the inspiratory reserve capacity. The total lung volume is the sum of the inspiratory reserve capacity plus the tidal volume and the functional residual volume.

The respiratory dead space is that volume occupied by gas which does not exchange with blood in the pulmonary vessels; it is therefore made up of the anatomical dead space of the trachea and bronchi plus the extra volume of the alveoli that do not contribute to gas exchange.

The vital capacity is the total amount of air that can be expired after a maximum inspiratory effort (i.e. the inspiratory reserve plus tidal volume plus expiratory reserve capacities; it is the latter which is described in part E).

The functional reserve capacity is the expiratory reserve plus the residual volume i.e. the amount of gas in the lungs at the end expiratory position. Both the expiratory reserve and the residual volume are reduced in pregnancy and hence the functional reserve is reduced by around 500 ml or 20% of non-pregnant values, at term.

22. **A E**

The term sex-linkage is virtually synonymous with X-linkage; the Y chromosome appears to have few loci apart from those determining the male sex. The only documented Y-linked state is that of the 'hairy pinna'.

Congenital ichthyosis is an X-linked disorder associated with a steroid sulphatase deficiency (and hence may be associated with very low oestriol levels in pregnancy).

Hurler's syndrome is determined by an autosomal recessive gene and achondroplasia by an autosomal dominant. Cleft palate, whether or not associated with cleft lip, seems to have a multifactorial inheritance pattern.

23. **A B D E**
Diazoxide produces a strong dilatation and is useful for the acute lowering of blood pressure. It binds heavily to plasma proteins and must therefore be given by rapid intravenous bolus injection; its effects last for several hours. It leads long-term to sodium and water retention (due to renin release) and is not therefore suitable for long-term use. It has a much greater effect on the B-cells than the thiazides, to which group it is related chemically.

24. **A B D**
Labetolol combines a non-selective beta-adrenoceptor blocking action with peripheral, postsynaptic alpha-adrenoceptor blockade, resulting in an intensification of the hypotension produced by each mechanism. Postural hypotension is relatively uncommon (an especial advantage in pregnancy). It has a more rapid onset of the beta-antagonistic depressor effect, as immediate reflex alpha-vasoconstriction is reduced. There is a negligible incidence of cold extremities as alpha-vasoconstriction is reduced.

25. **B C D E**
The obturator nerve has a root value of L2, 3, 4 (as does the femoral nerve). On passing through the obturator foramen, the nerve divides into an anterior and posterior division which supplies the six adductors. The sole anterior branch is the continuation of the nerve to gracilis. It reaches the surface about the middle of the thigh, where it supplies a restricted area, but it may extend to the calf. Articular branches supply both the hip and knee joints.

26. **B D E**
The sex chromosome trisomy 47XXY is known as Klinefelter's syndrome. Mongolism, or Down's syndrome, is a trisomy of autosome

21. The Barr body represents the inactive X chromosome material adjacent to the nuclear membrane in normal female cells; in any genotype with more than one X chromosome the additional chromosome will be present as Barr bodies, one for each additional X; thus XXY individuals have one Barr body, XXXY 2 Barr bodies etc. Such individuals usually develop gynaecomastia at puberty and are infertile, having under-developed testes. Older individuals are frequently mentally subnormal.

27. **A D**

Mitosis is the process in eukaryotic cells by which chromosomes are distributed at cell division. It consists of condensation of the duplicated chromosomes during prophase, movement of the chromosomes to the central region of the cell at metaphase, separation of the duplicated parts of each chromosome to separate sides of the cell in anaphase and formation of daughter nuclei by decondensation of the chromosomes and formation of the nuclear envelope in telophase. At the end of telophase the cell undergoes cytokinesis, forming two daughter cells.

The number of chromosomes is constant in the cells of any given species and therefore the number of different DNA double helices is constant. Prophase in mammalian cells typically takes 20 to 30 minutes. In other species, for example amphibians and plants, prophase may take several hours.

Most kinds of cancer cell have more than 46 chromosomes, some of which cannot be matched into pairs. Such cells are said to be aneuploid.

28. **B**

Arginine vasopressin, antidiuretic hormone, is produced by cell bodies in the supraoptic and paraventricular nuclei of the hypothalamus and is stored and released from the posterior pituitary. It is an octapeptide (although having a cystine molecule, made up of two cysteine residues joined by a disulphide bond it is referred to as a nonapeptide in some texts). It increases the permeability of the distal tubule and collecting ducts to water and therefore increases reabsorption and decreases urine volume. Its release is controlled by changes in plasma osmolality and plasma volume, the osmoreceptors being in the hypothalamus although the location of volume receptors is uncertain. Deficiency of vasopressin causes the clinical picture of diabetes insipidus; alcohol inhibits vasopressin release.

29. **B C**

The standard deviation of a series of observations is a measure of the extent of their spread about their mean. It is calculated from the mean and the number of observations but each individual observation must also be known. It is used in several tests of significance but is not in itself a measure of significance. It is only meaningful for observations that have a normal, Gaussian distribution and in such populations may be used to predict centiles e.g. mean ± 1 s.d. includes 68% of the population therefore mean - 1 s.d. includes 68% of population therefore mean - 1 s.d. is equivalent to the 16th centile and mean + 1 s.d. to the 84th centile; the standard deviation is however not synonymous with a centile.

30. **A**

Amniotic fluid volume rises with gestation to around 36 weeks, volumes being approximately 30 ml at 10 weeks, 250 ml at 20 weeks, 750 ml at 30 weeks and 900 ml at 36 weeks; thereafter liquor volume falls slightly to around 800 ml at term. Up to midpregnancy the amniotic fluid has a composition similar to fetal extracellular fluid and its volume is closely related to fetal weight. During the second half of pregnancy the fetal skin keratinises and continuity between fetal extracellular fluid and the amniotic cavity is lost; fetal urine production then provides a large contribution to amniotic fluid volume and hence the creatinine content progressively increases and osmolality falls with advancing gestation. Liquor alphafetoprotein level falls from 14 weeks to term.

31. **A C**

Translation occurs in the nucleus, but is smaller than heterogeneous RNA which contains sequences representing introns. The sugar moiety of mesenger RNA is ribose rather than deoxyribose. It is not manufactured until after the first cleavage division. Prior to that, metabolism in the embryo depends on residual RNA from the oocyte cytoplasm. Three bases constitute the codon.

32. **D E**

The primary yolk sac is formed from the blastocyst cavity when mesoderm appears between cytotrophoblast and extra-embryonic endoderm. The secondary yolk sac is formed from the collapsed primary sac when the extra-embryonic coelom forms within the extra-embryonic mesoderm. The primitive streak develops in the bilaminar disk at about 14 days. The syncytiotrophoblast forms and can begin secretion of specific products such as HCG. Monozygotic twins arise from fission of a single embryo soon after implantation.

33. **B C E**
Candida albicans is a fungus commensal in the human gastrointestinal tract. It is an opportunistic pathogen and host defences usually have to be weakened before infection occurs: diabetics, alcoholics, drug addicts, those with anaemias or leukaemias in addition to pregnant or pill-taking women are particularly prone to infection. The organism may be identified microscopically by the large budding yeast cells with long pseudohyphae; flagellae are not present. Culture of suspected specimens should be carried out on Sabouraud's medium. Nystatin, in the form of cream or pessary is usually effective treatment; failure may be due to reinfection from the bowel and oral treatment should be given concurrently.

34. **A C D**
Vitamin K exists in nature in two forms K1 and K2, both derivatives of the cyclic structure naphthoquinone, which is fat soluble. Vitamin K is readily synthesised by *Escherichia coli* and other gastrointestinal commensals and hence primary dietary deficiency never arises in man. When long-term broad spectrum antibiotics are used the disturbance in bowel flora may lead to deficiency. Its main function is in formation of coagulation factors II, VII, IX and X by the liver; deficiency may therefore be associated with haemorrhagic phenomena especially in the premature newborn whose liver function may be immature.

35. **A C D E**
The Mullerian duct (paramesonephric duct) arises as a groove in the mesonephric ridge, lateral to the mesonephric duct. The groove becomes tubular by the fusion of the two edges of the invagination.

The upper part forms the Fallopian tube and its cranial end remains open into the peritoneal cavity. The free caudal end of the Mullerian duct crosses the mesonephric duct and approaches the urogenital sinus. On the dorsal wall of the sinus the two ducts fuse to form the

Mullerian cord which will become the uterus and cervix. The mesonephric or Wolffian ducts are concerned with epididymis and vas deferens formation in the male. The primitive urogenital sinus does receive the mesonephric ducts and is continuous along the mesonephric openings with the allantois. The lower part of the vagina may develop from canalization of the sino-vaginal bulbs.

36. **A C**
The total red cell mass, in the absence of iron supplementation, increases by around 18%; the increase appears to be approximately linear from the end of the first trimester up to term. The plasma volume increases by approximately 40% in healthy primigravid patients; this increase is greater in multigravidae and in multiple pregnancy and less in association with fetal growth impairment and pregnancy-induced hypertension. The mean corpuscular haemoglobin concentration does not change significantly in normal pregnancy, or in folate deficiency. The mean red cell volume changes little in normal pregnancy; values less than 80 fl are highly suggestive of iron deficiency, the reduction in MCV occurring before any change in MCHC. The total white cell count increases in pregnancy, due largely to an increase in neutrophils.

37. **A B E**
Tuberculosis of the female genital tract most commonly occurs by haematogenous spread following primary pulmonary infection. Whilst 10% of women with genital tuberculosis will have had previous pregnancies, subsequent infertility may be a feature in up to 70%. Tuberculosis of the lung and renal tract occurs with the same frequency during pregnancy as at other times.

The principles of antibiotic therapy for tuberculosis traditionally are that three drugs to which the organisms are fully sensitive should be used for three months and thereafter only two drugs need to be continued for a minimum of nine months. More recently, regimens of shorter duration (6 months) have been advocated, but at least two drugs must be employed.

38. **B C D**
Malignant tumours often have a cell production rate greater than adjacent normal tissue, but not invariably so. In particular, gut carcinomas often have a proliferation rate less than adjacent normal

gut mucosa. Metastasis is characteristic of malignant tumours, but this tendency varies according to site; cervical carcinoma rarely metastasises to liver or bone whereas bronchial carcinoma more frequently does so, for example.

Malignant tumours are characteristically aneuploid and most are sensitive to irradiation, but damage to adjacent normal tissue often limits therapeutic potential. Not all malignant tumours are poorly differentiated. A good example of an exception is the so-called 'minimal-deviation adenocarcinoma of the cervix', a very well differentiated tumour with great metastatic potential.

39. **C D**

The gonococcus is a Gram-negative intracellular diplococcus which does not exist in an anerobic form. Infection may have a bacteraemic phase with resultant gonococcal arthritis or endocarditis; the more usual sites of infection in the female however are the endocervix, endosalpinx, urethra, rectum, pharynx and Bartholin's glands. Up to 1976 all strains were penicillin sensitive although since then increasing reports of beta-lactamase producing, penicillin resistant organisms have appeared.

40. **A D**

Cytotoxic drugs exert their effects predominantly on rapidly-dividing cells and they may therefore affect fetal development and cause abortion or congenital malformation when used in the first trimester; this risk is greatest with folic acid antagonists such as methotrexate and alkylating agents such as cyclophosphamide. Penicillin readily crosses the placenta but appears to be entirely safe for use in pregnancy. Heparin does not cross the placenta and is thus non-teratogenic. Testosterone may cause virilisation of a female fetus with clitoral hypertrophy and labial fusion if given to a mother in early pregnancy; other studies suggest an increased incidence of other congenital malformations including cardiovascular abnormalities, limb defects and neural tube defects. Barbiturates have been used as sedatives in pregnancy for over 50 years and although there have been sporadic reports of abnormality there is no convincing evidence of significant teratogenicity.

41. **B C**

Parathormone is secreted by the so-called transitional cells of the parathyroid glands; the thyroid C-cells produce calcitonin. The control of parathormone secretion is by alterations in the ionised calcium level in the blood, an increase in Ca^{2+} (other than from primary hyperparathyroidism) leading to a reduction in hormone output. Hypomagnesaemia also leads to a decrease in parathormone secretion although it is unlikely that this effect is of physiological significance. The effects of parathormone are to produce hypercalcaemia, hypophosphataemia and hypercalcuria and increased urinary hydroxyproline excretion; these changes result from increased bone resorption, decreased tubular reabsorption of phosphate and increased absorption of calcium in the gastrointestinal tract. Parathormone has no effect on the pituitary.

42. **C**

Cytology is the examination of dispersed cells rather than pieces of tissue; exfoliative cytology examines cells which have been shed or scraped from an epithelial surface. Fine-needle aspiration cytology is useful for organs which do not have easily accessible epithelial surfaces. The main use of exfoliative cytology in Britain is in the national screening programme for cervical carcinoma. Cells are scraped from the cervix with a spatula and then spread on slides before staining with Papanicolou stain, after which cytological examination is carried out. Exfoliative cytology is of no value in screening for ovarian carcinoma.

The cytological diagnosis of breast lesions is usually made on samples obtained by fine-needle aspiration. Cytology of shed cells in nipple discharge has not proved very useful.

43. **A B**

Toxic shock syndrome is caused by an exotoxin which is produced by *Staphylococcus aureus*. Syphilis is caused by the spirochaete *Treponema pallidum*. Infectious mononucleosis is caused by infection with the Epstein-Barr virus. Rubella is caused by a togavirus and rabies by a rhabdovirus.

44. **A D E**

Fibroblasts are very important cells in the process of repair. Granulation tissue derives its name from the granular appearance of the base of a skin ulcer. Granulomas are not an integral part of granulation tissue but may be present if there is foreign material or an infectious agent which elicits a granulomatous response. Liver cells are capable of rapid regeneration, so healing by repair is an uncommon event in the liver unless the injury is persistent or repetitive. Some of the fibroblasts differentiate into myofibroblasts, so active contraction of the granulation tissue is possible.

45. **A B C E**
Following haemorrhage, not only are there changes which reduce the capacity of the circulation, but also some which increase the filling. Fluid moves into the cardiovascular system from the interstitium; the fall in blood pressure and the accompanying arteriolar vasoconstriction results in a fall in the capillary hydrostatic pressure and hence the filtering pressure and the fluid lost from the cardiovascular system is reduced. This leads to a dilution of the plasma proteins, a change which would however reduce the fluid uptake. This capillary mechanism only results in redistribution of the extracellular fluid. To reduce fluid loss, the fall in blood pressure contributes to reduced glomerular filtration rate and oliguria. The decreased blood volume also leads to an elevation of vasopressin and hence enhanced fluid retention. There is also increased renin release from the renal juxtaglomerular apparatus and hence of angiotensin II formation, resulting in increased output of aldosterone from the adrenal cortex. This leads to a positive sodium balance and hence increased extracellular fluid volume. Inhibition of release of atrial natriuretic peptide may also reduce sodium output and contribute to the positive sodium balance.

46. **A B C D E**
Colostrum has a higher protein content than milk, but contains less fat and carbohydrate. The onset and maintenance of lactation is due to prolactin. High concentrations of progesterone will inhibit lactation (as during pregnancy). Oxytocin is not required for milk formation, but is essential for milk ejection.

47. **A C**
Thyroxine, or tetra-iodothyronine, is produced by coupling of two molecules of the iodinated tyrosine derivative di-iodotyrosine. It circulates largely in bound form to the plasma protein thyroid binding globulin, thyroid binding pre-albumin and albumin, only 0.04% being

in the free form. Among the biological effects of thyroxine are its stimulant effect on growth and development, both overall growth and maturation of specific tissues being effective. It leads to an increased oxygen consumption and heat production, as recorded by an increase in basal metabolic rate; brain, spleen, testis, uterus and anterior pituitary do not increase oxygen consumption in response to increased thyroxine levels. Serum cholesterol is lowered in hyperthyroidism and raised in hypothyroidism.

48. **D E**

Cytotoxic drugs do not kill tumour cells directly but affect cell division and thereby cell proliferation. Alkylating agents such as cyclophosphamide transfer alkyl groups to biologically important cell constituents such as amino, carboxyl sulphydryl or phosphate groups whose function is then impaired. 5-fluorouracil is an antimetabolite which interferes with the synthesis of nucleic acids. Plant alkaloids such as vincristine and vinblastine produce mitotic arrest by binding to a cytoplasmic precursor of the spindle. Many of the antibiotics such as adriamycin bind selectively to DNA, forming complexes that block the formation of DNA-dependent RNA. Tamoxifen acts by blocking oestrogen receptors (which in hormone-dependent cancers stimulate growth) but can have some cytotoxic effect even in the absence of oestrogens.

49. **A B C E**

An embolus is a 'foreign' material transported from one part of the circulatory system to another, whence it becomes impacted. The most usual form of embolus is a thrombus formed in the heart or blood vessel wall, which becomes detached. Other types of emboli include air (usually from iatrogenic causes), fat, (often following fracture of a long bone), tumour (by direct invasion of the circulation by malignant cells, or by dissemination at the time of surgery) and amniotic fluid (following rupture of membranes especially during rapid labour). Urinary, biliary or salivary calculi cannot enter the circulation and therefore cannot form emboli.

50. **A B E**

Micturition is dependent on a spinal reflex arc mediated via parasympathetic efferents and accompanying visceral afferents and accompanying visceral afferent fibres synapsing within the conus medullaris at spinal level S2-4. Normal coordinated micturition is of course also dependent on higher central control involving additional relay centres in the pontine reticular formation (for the coordination of detrusor contraction with urethral relaxation), the basal ganglion (for subconscious inhibition of micturition) and in the paracentral lobule and superior frontal gyrus of the cerebral cortex (for the appreciation of the desire to void, conscious inhibition and then subsequent voluntary initiation of voiding). It is these latter cortical centres which give the detrusor its property, unique among smooth muscles, of being under voluntary control. Any neurological lesion below the pontine centre will lead to a discoordinate voiding pattern, with urethral contraction accompanying detrusor contraction and thus a residual volume is likely to remain after voiding.

The lower urinary tract has a sympathetic nerve supply from spinal segments T12 to L2; this seems to be of greater relevance to the filling and storage phases of the micturition cycle than to voiding itself and transection of these fibres has little influence on micturition.

51. A E
The ovarian artery on each side is a branch of the abdominal aorta just below the level of the renal arteries. The ovarian veins form a plexus in the mesovarium and infundibulo-pelvic ligament; a pair of veins on each side usually combine into a single trunk before their termination; that on the right joins the inferior vena cava and that on the left, the left renal vein (this is embryologically symmetrical since on each side the vein concerned is a persistent part of the subcardinal vein of the embryo). The ovary is covered by a single layered cuboidal epithelium, the so-called germinal epithelium; it is attached to the posterior aspect of the broad ligament. The suspensory ligament of the ovary connects the medial pole of the ovary to the uterine fundus, being part of the gubernaculum.

52. A B C D
The Fallopian tubes develop from the unfused rostral portions of the paramesonephric or Mullerian ducts. The calibre of the tube varies along its length being maximal in the ampullary region and minimal in the isthmus. The fimbria ovarica attaches the tube to the lateral pole of the ovary and presumably aids ovum transport into the tube following ovulation. The tubal lining is a single layered columnar epithelium

containing ciliated secretory and resting or peg cells; the secretory cells develop microvilli and become secretory at midcycle and ciliary activity also increases at ovulation.

53. **C D**

The vagina develops in part from the paramesonephric or Mullerian ducts and in part from the urogenital sinus; the relative proportions of these two contributions are disputed. The epithelium of the vagina is a non-keratinising stratified squamous epithelium The posterior relations of the vagina are the pouch of Douglas in the upper third, the rectum in the middle third and the perineal body in the lower third. The vaginal blood supply is from descending branches of the uterine arteries (upper third), lateral continuations of the inferior vesical arteries and terminal branches of the internal iliac arteries (middle third) and from the ascending clitoral arteries (lower third).

54. **A D**

The breast is an ectodermal structure developing from a downward growth of epidermis into the underlying mesenchyme, in a similar manner to which sweat glands develop, but occurring specifically along two thickened strips of ectoderm, the mammary ridges. Branching epithelial cords appear, become canalised in midgestation and further proliferation and branching occurs up to full term and again at puberty. Lobular organisation within the breast occurs at puberty with the development ultimately of 15-20 lobes each of which drains into a single lactiferous duct which opens via the lactiferous sinus onto the surface of the nipple; true secretory alveoli do not appear until the woman herself becomes pregnant. Although the mature breast varies greatly in size, its base is fairly constant, extending from the 2nd to 6th ribs in the midclavicular line and overlying pectoralis major, serratus anterior and external oblique. The lymphatic drainage of the superficial parts of the breast is into a subareolar plexus and of the deep parts into a submammary plexus, which communicate freely with each other and with the opposite side. From these plexi, lymph drains laterally to the pectoral group of axillary glands and inferiorly via lymph glands in the anterior abdominal wall through the diaphragm and on to the mediastinal glands.

55. A D E

Human leucocyte antigens are present on most nucleated cells. Two antigens are inherited from each parent making a total of four. Homozygosity may result in only two defined antigens being present but this is not the usual situation. In man, the transplantation antigens are determined by a number of genes situated at independent loci. The antigens determined by these gene complexes are termed the HLA antigens. It is thought that a combination of humoral and cellular factors is responsible for homograft rejection.

56. A B

Clinical trials are usually controlled in that they invariably utilise a group of patients receiving a standard treatment or no active treatment as a comparative gauge to evaluate the effect of a new treatment. An uncontrolled trial provides a distorted view of therapy. Randomisation is usually adopted as a mechanism for overcoming bias.

The use of historical controls is acceptable and has the advantage that all patients in the trial receive the new treatment which the investigators expect to be superior. The number required for the trial is thereby reduced. However such studies are susceptible to biases introduced by changes in the nature of the patient population.

There is no minimum number for a clinical trial, nor must trials always be double-blind, although these help to reduce subjective bias on the part of the patient or trial organiser.

57. A D E

The femoral sheath is an investment of extraperitoneal fascia extending over the femoral artery and vein as they pass beneath the inguinal ligament; the vein lies medial to the artery in the sheath but medial to the vein lies a space, the femoral canal. Lymph vessels from the inguinal nodes pass through this space which also contains the node of Cloquet. The canal is widest at its proximal end where its opening is known as the femoral ring; this is bounded anteriorly by the inguinal ligament, medially by the lacular ligament and laterally by the femoral vein. The femoral branch of the genito-femoral nerve passes in front of the femoral artery to pierce the femoral sheath and fascia lata and thus lies well lateral to the femoral canal.

58. **A B D E**

The typical female pelvic shape in the UK has a brim which is slightly wider in its transverse than A-P diameter (gynaecoid), the true obstetric conjugate being 11-12 cm and the transverse 13 cm. The cavity has the contours of a curved cylinder rather than a funnel, the side walls being approximately parallel. The greater sciatic notch is usually greater than 90° and the subpubic angle should also approximate to a right angle.

59. **A D E**

Krebs cycle is also called the citric acid cycle and produces, by oxidation, metabolic energy in the form of ATP. It is the process responsible for harnessing the contained chemical energy in carbohydrates, but it is not purely catabolic, facilitating as it does the synthesis of essential metabolites such as amino-acids and long-chain fatty acids. The cycle depends upon a continuous supply of oxidised co-enzyme for its maintenance and does allow the complete combustion of fatty acids.

60. **A B D**

Vitamin B12 is produced by moulds and fungi but is absent from all other plant products; the main dietary sources are liver, meat, eggs and milk. Like other B vitamins it is water soluble and is not destroyed by cooking. Daily requirements are quite low (1 to 3 micrograms daily and this is met by all but the most strictly vegetarian diets). Deficiency is characterised by a macrocyctic megaloblastic anaemia and this is usually due to impaired absorption rather than dietary deficiency. Absorption of B12 occurs in the ileum and is dependent on the presence of 'intrinsic factor', a glycoprotein produced by the gastric mucosa. In true Addisonian pernicious anaemia or in gastrectomised patients the deficiency of intrinsic factor must be circumvented by parenteral administration of B12.

ANSWERS TO PRACTICE EXAM 2

1. **A B E**
    The cervical mucus at ovulation appears as a copious transparent fluid in contrast to the rest of the cycle when it is scanty and opalescent; the cervical mucus is alkaline. Fructose is a reducing sugar which provides the chief form of energy for spermatozoa under anaerobic conditions. There is no evidence that semen is 'sucked' into the uterus at coitus. It is believed by some that a retroverted uterus with the cervix pointing towards the anterior vaginal wall may be a factor in infertility by reducing contact with the seminal pool.

2. **B D E**
    Prostaglandins are fatty acids, found in prostatic fluid but predominantly produced by the seminal vesicles. They induce rhythmic uterine contractions and are used for induction of labour or ripening of the cervix. Prostaglandins tend to produce diarrhoea, not constipation. Aspirin acts by inhibiting the synthesis of prostaglandins as the latter are thought to be responsible for inflammation, pain and pyrexia. Bronchospasm is rare, but may occur with PgF2alpha; care is therefore required in asthmatic patients.

3. **C**
    There is no evidence that maternal growth hormone positively influences birth weight. Primiparity and social class are not consistently related to birth weight.

4. **B E**
    Glandular neoplasia is less common than its squamous counterpart, but it has been underdiagnosed in the past and is often detected as an incidental finding perhaps as a result of carrying out a cone biopsy for CIN. Indeed, the two not infrequently co-exist, raising the likelihood of origin from common stem cells. Adenocarcinoma of the cervix is thought to be the precursor of invasive adenocarcinoma and both are certainly increasing in incidence. The reason for this is unclear; the oral contraceptive pill has been suggested as a possible aetiological agent, but the evidence for this is not convincing. Because the abnormal glandular cells may be high up the endocervical canal, abnormalities are less easily detected then squamous abnormalities.

5. **A C**

    Androstenedione is converted to oestrone by aromatase, which is an enzyme in fat cells and the oestrone may stimulate endometrial hyperplasia. Unopposed oestrogenic stimulation may lead to simple or occasionally complex hyperplasia and it is the latter which may progress to invasive carcinoma. Endometrial hyperplasia is a histological diagnosis made on clinical examination of endometrial curettings. It is more common in pre- and perimenopausal women.

6. **A C D E**

    Fibroids are associated with low parity. Submucous fibroids may distort the uterine cavity and interfere with embryo implantation, which may also result in an increase in the surface area of the uterine cavity and lead to menorrhagia. Fibroids are often multiple and may reach enormous sizes.

7. **B C D E**

    Gynaecomastia occurs most frequently at puberty and in old age. Gynaecomastia is associated with hyperthyroidism, pituitary disorders and adrenal or testicular tumours. Stilboestrol has been used to treat prostatic carcinoma and this may lead to gynaecomastia.

8. **D E**

    The Fallopian tube exhibits four types of epithelial cell, ciliated, secretory, intercalary (or peg) cells and basal cells probably used in regeneration. Ciliated cells are most numerous in the region of the infundibulum and ampulla, with secretory cells more often found in the isthmus. There are three muscle layers. The fertilised egg remains in the tube for three or four days. The epithelium exhibits cyclical variation in response to oestrogen and progestogen levels; an optimum ratio is thought to be required to ensure passage of the oocyte towards the uterus. There is no clear demarcation between the isthmus and ampulla.

9. **A B D**

    There are rich venous communications with the dorsal veins of the clitoris. Lymphatic systems cross-connect (contralateral groin nodes may be affected by a tumour of the labium majus).

10. **C E**
The ureter is lined with transitional epithelium and has three muscle layers only. It passes down the psoas muscle crossing the bifurcation of the common iliac artery. From here it passes below the uterine artery to cross the lateral fornix of the vagina and enter the bladder in front of the vagina. The ureter possesses a longitudinal anastamosing network of arteries derived from the renal artery and aorta above and the gonadal and vesical arteries below; it is of mesodermal origin.

11. **A B**
The trigone is relatively fixed and non-distensible. The ureters pierce the muscle and mucosal walls obliquely. The epithelium of the trigone arises from mesoderm.

12. **A B E**
The ischial spines are on the posterior border of the ischium and demarcate an upper (greater) and lower (lesser) sciatic notch. They are normally not particularly prominent in the female pelvis; if they are they may lead to reduction of the interspinous diameter and arrest of the fetal skull. When the head is at the level of the spines, it is deeply engaged.

13. **A C**
The right ovary receives its blood supply from the abdominal aorta, the ovarian artery arising at the level of the renal arteries. The veins on the right side drain to the inferior vena cava, but on the left, to the left renal vein. The ovary is attached to the back of the broad ligament by the mesovarium. The lower pole of the ovary is attached to the lateral margin of the uterus by the ovarian ligament. There is no peritoneal covering of the ovary in the adult.

14. **A D**
The uterine artery passes above the ureter in the broad ligament (think of 'water under the bridge'). It supplies the cervix via a descending branch. It forms an anastomosis with the tubal branch of the ovarian artery. The round ligament is supplied by the ovarian artery in the broad ligament and by the inferior epigastric artery in the inguinal canal.

15. **A B C D**

The internal iliac artery is a terminal branch of the common iliac artery. It has four visceral and seven parietal branches:

Visceral 1. Superior vesical artery
2. Uterine artery supplies vagina, uterus and tubes and anastomoses with the ovarian artery which arises directly from the aorta
3. Middle rectal artery
4. Vaginal artery supplies vagina, bladder and ureter

Parietal 1. Umbilical artery obliterates soon after birth
2. Obturator artery
3. Internal pudendal artery
4. Inferior gluteal artery
5. Superior gluteal artery
6. Lateral sacral artery
7. Iliolumbar artery

16. **A D E**

The pudendal nerve is part of the sacral plexus and arises from sacral nerve roots S2, S3, S4. It enters the gluteal region through the greater sciatic foramen on the medial side of the corresponding vessels. After crossing the ischial spine the nerve re-enters the pelvis through the lesser sciatic foramen. The pudendal nerve gives off the inferior rectal nerve and ends by dividing into the perineal nerve and the dorsal nerve of the clitoris.

17. **A B D**

The femoral nerve arises from the posterior divisions of the 2nd, 3rd and 4th lumbar nerves. It descends in the groove between iliacus and psoas, passes deep to the inguinal ligament and enters the thigh on the lateral side of the femoral artery which in turn is lateral to the femoral vein. The femoral sheath is a tube-like continuation of the extraperitoneal fascia into the thigh; the aorta and its branches along with the inferior vena cava and its tributaries lie within the fascial envelope while the spinal nerves emerge from the intervertebral foramina behind it.

18. **D**

The commonest blood group is O rhesus-positive (only 15% of the European population are rhesus-negative). There are no A or B antigens on the red cells and during the first year of life antibodies are produced against antibodies not present on the surface of the red cells. If a transfusion is required, only O rhesus-negative blood should be given, otherwise the antibodies present in the blood will attack the antigens present on the surface of the transfused cells. Following childbirth, anti-D immunoglobulin should only be given if the baby is rhesus-positive, to block the development of maternal antibodies to the rhesus-positive cells, which may attack fetal red cells in a subsequent pregnancy.

19. **A B C**

The steroid hormones are derived from cholesterol and are produced by the adrenal cortex and the gonads. Vitamin D is formed in the skin and then metabolised in the liver and kidney, giving the active derivative 1,25 dihydroxycholecalciferol which then acts on target organs, via the blood stream.

20. **A E**

Rhesus isoimmunisation is less common in ABO incompatible pregnancies as fetal red cells in the maternal circulation are coated with antibody much more quickly when ABO incompatibility exists and so sensitisation is less likely to be produced. 2 to 4% of Rh-ve women develop anti-D antibodies during their first pregnancy, but 25% of those mothers exposed to rhesus antigen will respond with antibody production. The commonest responsible rhesus antigen is D. The antigen is usually an intrinsic part of the red cell membrane. Cell bound antibodies are not able to cross the placenta to inflict haemolysis on the fetus; the responsible antibodies are the IgG group.

21. **C D E**

Vitamin B12 is the 'extrinsic factor' present in the diet, which cannot be absorbed from the small intestine unless the mucoprotein ('intrinsic factor') is elaborated by the appropriate cells in the gastric mucosa, which are non-functional in pernicious anaemia. The vitamin is present only in animal tissues and is therefore absent from plants (vegans are susceptible to pernicious anaemia). In pernicious anaemia the difficulty of absorption of the vitamin can be overcome by the parenteral administration of cyanocobalamin or preferably, injections of the longer-lasting hydroxocobalamin. Folic acid and vitamin B12 act together to achieve erythropoiesis, but are antagonistic in the formation of myelin.

22. **B C**
Glucose transfer takes place by facilitated diffusion and eventually becomes saturated. Fructose is not an 'aldose' sugar and therefore does not take part in the transfer mechanism. There is only a very small concentration gradient across the placenta.

23. **A D**
Renin is a protein of molecular weight 65,000. It is produced mainly in the kidney but in small amounts in other tissues such as the uterus and salivary glands. Cells in the juxtaglomerular apparatus of the kidney are sensitive to changes in pressure in the afferent arteriole. A fall in blood pressure stimulates renin release which leads to production of angiotensin II and aldosterone. Aldosterone enhances reabsorption of sodium and a decrease in blood sodium concentration and/or a rise in potassium will stimulate aldosterone release. Potassium secretion in association with sodium reabsorption occurs in the distal tubular epithelium.

24. **A B D**
There are normally 4,000-11,000 white blood cells per ml of human blood. Monocytes are usually larger than other peripheral blood leucocytes. Only 1% of the polymorphonuclear leucocytes in females have a drum-stick appendage attached to one of the lobes; this may represent the inactive X chromosome. Lymphocytes do have a basophilic cyloplasm when mature. Eosinophils constitute only a very small proportion (%) of the white cell count under normal conditions. The packed cell volume is slightly lower in women, being in the range 36-48%, compared to 40-52% seen in men.

25. **A B**
HCG is detectable in maternal serum around the time of implantation of the ovum at 5-6 days post-ovulation but within the present limitations of sensitivity of radioimmunassay it has not yet been possible to demonstrate HCG prior to this time, because of the close structural similarity between HCG and LH the two hormones are very similar in

their biological and immunological properties. One of the major roles for HCG is its stimulus to sustain the functioning corpus luteum, converting it into the corpus luteum of pregnancy. There exists no evidence to implicate HCG in the initiation of parturition, maternal serum concentration altering little in late pregnancy. No association has been shown with pre-eclampsia.

26. **A C E**
The fetal zone of the adrenal cortex comprises approximately 80% of the gland in fetal life; after birth these cells undergo involution and disappear by 6 months of age. Human growth hormone is produced in utero by the fetal pituitary gland, maximal secretion occurring between 20 and 24 weeks. The fetus near term can respond to a glucose load by increasing the serum concentration of insulin but the response is usually small except in the offspring of diabetic mothers. The intermediate lobe of the pituitary gland is more prominent in the fetus than in the adult in whom it is not well represented or understood. Chromaffin cells, which contain noradrenaline, are found in the adrenal medulla, but also around the aorta, in the skin and throughout the alimentary tract. During fetal life and early childhood chromaffin cells are abundant. By the second year of life they atrophy but may be detectable for several years as the organ of Zuckercandl.

27. **B D E**
Oxytocin is a polypeptide consisting of eight amino acids. It is synthesised in the paraventricular nuclei of the hypothalamus. It passes down the axons of the pituitary stalk to reach the posterior lobe of the pituitary whence its release is controlled principally by nerve impulses from the hypothalamus. It differs in only two amino acid residues from vasopressin (antidiuretic hormone), also synthesised in the hypothalamus and stored in the posterior pituitary. Because of this, oxytocin has some antidiuretic properties. The uterus in early pregnancy is not very sensitive to oxytocin, but the latter may be used as a synergistic agent (with prostaglandin) in therapeutic abortion.

28. **A C D**
Progesterone is a steroid hormone which is formed in the ovary, placenta, adrenal gland and testis. All the steroid hormones are synthesised from acetate or acetyl co-enzyme A. The early synthetic steps are common to all steroids and involve the formation of

cholesterol. Progesterone after secretion becomes largely bound to carrier plasma proteins. It is degraded mainly in the liver and a small fraction appears in the urine as the inactive conjugate pregnanediol glucuronide. The main source of 17- hydroxyprogesterone hormone in the menstrual cycle and in early pregnancy is the corpus luteum but after 6-8 weeks of pregnancy the vast majority of progesterone is elaborated by the placenta. In pregnancy and probably during the menstrual cycle one of its actions is to reduce the excitability of the myometrium.

29. **A C D**

The prostaglandins are a group of chemically related 20 carbon-hydroxy fatty acid derivatives of prostanoic acid. It seems likely that they are synthesised in most and possibly all the organs of the body from arachidonic acid. The enzyme that converts arachidonic acid to acyclic endoperoxidase is inhibited by indomethacin. PgE2 augments platelet aggregation during coagulation. PgE2 will also stimulate the smooth muscle of the uterus and is used as an abortifacient and inductor of labour. It is not an antidiuretic.

30. **A B D E**

Interferons are glycoproteins produced by virus-infected cells. They are now widely available, produced by recombinant DNA technology. There is hope that they will prove useful in the management of viral infections and in treating certain malignancies and are particularly useful in the management of hairy-cell leukaemia.

31. **B D E**

Chlamydia trachomatis requires the use of host cell substrates for the synthesis of its own nucleic acids and proteins. Light microscopy is an unreliable method of diagnosis, better methods include enzyme-linked immunoassay (ELISA), direct immunofluorescence and culture. Many women are asymptomatic carriers, however examination of the cervix may reveal local signs of infection such as a mucopurulent discharge. Of babies born to mothers with genital chlamydia, 10-20% will develop a pneumonia and up to 50% may develop conjunctivitis.

32. **A E**

The causative agent is the human papilloma virus. Most patients present with genital warts between the ages of 16 and 26. Salicylic acid is used in the treatment of hand warts and veruccae but is not effective against genital warts, for which treatment options include podophyllin, trichloracetic acid, cryotherapy, diathermy and surgery. Genital warts usually increase in size and respond less well to treatment during pregnancy. Podophyllin is teratogenic and is therefore not used in pregnancy. The aetiology of cervical intraepithelial neoplasia is not clear but several factors are thought to contribute including smoking, early onset of sexual activity, multiple sexual partners and the presence of HPV types 16 or 18.

33. **E**

Heterosexual intercourse is the main means of transmission on a world-wide scale. HIV II is common only in West Africa. Most acute infections are asymptomatic but some patients do experience a transient 'glandular fever' type illness. The rate of transmission in Africa at present is thought to be about 40% and that in the UK 15%. The three methods of vertical transmission of the virus are transplacental, by infected blood products at parturition and by infected breast milk. Oral lesions consist of adherent white plaques which are found at the lateral aspects of the tongue and cheeks. Unlike the lesions of oral candidiasis the plaques cannot be removed by means of scraping with a wooden spatula.

34. **B C D E**

Large amounts of histamine are found in the anterior and posterior pituitary lobes and the hypothalamic median eminence. The mast cells contain most of the histamine in the posterior pituitary gland although this is not the case in other sites. Histamine causes contraction of visceral smooth muscle but relaxes vascular smooth muscle and increases capillary permeability. Histamine is, in part, responsible for the wheal part of the triple response. Histamine also has a potent stimulatory effect on gastric acid secretion and is present in high concentration in gastric mucosa.

35. **A**

The paramesonephric ducts of each side appear as invaginations of the coelomic epithelium into the mesenchyme lateral to the cranial extremity of the mesonephric duct. The caudal part of the female mesonephric ducts degenerate and may persist as the Gartner's ducts. The caudal part of the female Mullerian duct does not degenerate but fuses with its partner from the other side to form the utero-vaginal canal. The caudal tip of this canal eventually comes into contact with the dorsal wall of the urogenital sinus where it produces an elevation, the Mullerian tubercle. The utero-vaginal canal and cells derived from its lower end give rise to the epithelial lining of the uterus and possible part of the vagina. Proliferation of the tip of the utero-vaginal canal results in a solid vaginal cord which increases progressively the distance between the utero-vaginal lumen and the urogenital sinus. The vagina is thought to develop from canalisation of the sino-vaginal bulbs and the hymen is the portion which persists to a varying degree between the dilated canalised fused sino-vaginal bulbs and the urogenital sinus proper. The Mullerian tubercle is therefore much higher. Sertoli cells are derived from sex cord cells initially joined to and possibly originating from germinal epithelium, not primordial sex cells. While the testis begins to emerge morphologically after the 7th week, ovarian development is not apparent until after the 13th week.

36. **A C D E**

A trait transmitted as an autosomal recessive is expressed only in homozygotes, persons who have received the gene from both parents. Theoretically the offspring of carrier parents have a 1 in 4 chance of being affected; two will be heterozygous and phenotypically normal and one will be homozygous for the normal allele and phenotypically normal; the fourth will be affected. Males and females are equally likely to be affected. Since rare recessive genes are passed down in families, the risk of having affected children is higher if a carrier marries within the family group. A parent or a grandparent of an affected child may well be similarly afflicted.

37. **B**

The standard deviation is the square root of the variance and is a measure of the scatter of observations around the mean. The population or sample group of observations should have a normal or Gaussian distribution. The standard deviation is not used in calculating chi-squared. One standard deviation each side of the mean encompasses 66% of observations and two standard deviations 95%.

38. **B C**

Oxygenated blood returns from the placenta via the umbilical vein; the umbilical arteries carry deoxygenated blood from fetus to placenta.

The ductus venosus provides a direct route of flow for oxygenated blood from the umbilical vein to the inferior vena cava. The foramen ovale connects the atria, and is an oblique passage through the interatrial septum, which closes soon after birth due to the greater left atrial pressure closing the septum primum against the septum secundum. The ductus arteriosus is a wide channel linking the left pulmonary artery with the aorta and joins the aorta distal to the origin of the three branches of the aortic arch.

39. **D E**

Haemoglobin A is a protein with a molecular weight of 64,450; the globin portion has alpha and beta chains. HbA2 contains alpha and delta chains. Haemoglobin F (fetal) is similar to HbA except that the beta chains are replaced by gamma chains. Fetal haemoglobin has the higher affinity for oxygen. Approximately 0.3 g of haemoglobin are destroyed and synthesised every hour (6 g/day). Haem is an iron-containing porphyrin derivative.

40. **D E**

The absorption of ergometrine following intramuscular injection is unpredictable, and because of its local arteriospastic effect is certainly delayed in comparison to oxytocin; uterine contraction may not occur for up to five minutes following this route of administration. Because of this same arterioconstrictor effect acting generally following systemic absorption, hypertension may occur, and in pre-eclamptic patients this effect may lead to very marked elevation in blood pressure. Bradycardia and vomiting are common side-effects.

41. **A E**

The oocyte and spermatozoa usually come together in the ampulla or outer third of the Fallopian tube. The full diploid genetic constitution is restored by fertilization. At the early morula stage the conceptus is enclosed within the zona pellucida which is lost after the blastocyst stage. Oviductal cilia and possibly the musculature of the genital tract are the active transporters of the embryo rather than the morula itself. HCG can be detected by radioimmunoassay in maternal blood as early as 5 days after conception and in anticipation of implantation.

42. **D E**

The volume of amniotic fluid increases up to 36-37 weeks of pregnancy after which there is a decline. The pH of amniotic fluid is between 7.1 and 7.25 i.e. alkaline. Organic constituents are mainly proteins and protein derivatives from maternal plasma. The protein content does decrease from 26 weeks onwards. A decrease in amniotic fluid volume is seen in pre-eclampsia and intrauterine growth retardation.

43. **A B D E**

Calcium homeostasis is maintained by three hormones: 1,25 dihydroxycholecalciferol which increases calcium absorption from the upper small intestine, parathyroid hormone which mobilises calcium from bones and increases urinary phosphate excretion, and calcitonin, a calcium lowering hormone which inhibits bone resorption. Calcium absorption is decreased by phosphates in the diet which bind to form insoluble salts with calcium. Fat soluble vitamins like D are poorly absorbed in the absence of pancreatic lipase; thus in pancreatitis deficiencies can develop. This may also result from coeliac disease. A high protein diet increases calcium absorption.

44. **A B E**

Subnuclear vacuolation of the glandular epithelium usually occurs 24-36 hours after ovulation. The changes which are seen in the endometrium after ovulation (secretory phase) are influenced by both oestrogens and progestogens. At the end of the secretory phase the walls of the spiral arteries constrict, causing ischaemia and necrosis of the endothelium. Rupture of the blood vessels above the constriction takes place and bleeding with desquamation of the functional layer of the endometrium occurs. Gland mitoses continue to occur in menstruating endometrium. Subsequent to shedding, endometrial regeneration occurs from the zona basilis.

45. **B**

The median of a series of observations is the centre value when the observations are ranged in order from highest to the lowest. The sum total of values divided by the number of observations is the mean. The value occurring most often is the mode or modal value. The distance between the highest and lowest values is the range. The square root of the standard deviation has no specific meaning.

46. **A C**

Streptococci are Gram-positive but they may be aerobic or anaerobic. They are spherical or oval cocci with a tendency to form chains rather than clusters. If *S. viridans*, a normal commensal of mouth and pharynx, gains access to the blood stream, particularly during dental filling or extraction, in patients with existing heart disease it can cause subacute bacterial endocarditis. Staphylococci are the organisms which produce coagulase.

47. **A C D**

Alpha-fetoprotein (AFP) is synthesised in the yolk-sac, the fetal liver and the fetal gastrointestinal tract early in pregnancy. Amniotic fluid levels follow the same trend as fetal serum levels. However, in maternal serum, AFP concentrations show a very different pattern; there is a gradual rise up to 34-36 weeks of pregnancy after which there is a gradual decline to term and a very rapid drop after delivery. There is little correlation between maternal serum levels and amniotic fluid concentration. Elevation of the maternal serum AFP is seen in twins, open neural tube defects, exomphalos and congenital nephrosis. Intrauterine death, where the normal integrity of the placenta (which blocks the transfer of AFP) is lost, also results in a rise in AFP. No rise has been demonstrated in association with congenital heart disease and microcephaly.

48. **C E**

TRH is a tripeptide (pyroglutamyl-histidyl-proline-amide). Human molar thyrotrophin has a far higher molecular weight than pituitary TSH. The amount of T4 in free form in plasma is 4 times greater than T3 but because the metabolic activity of the latter is 4 times that of T4 the contributions of free T4 and free T3 would be approximately equal in biological activity. 0.024% of thyroxine is normally in the free form. Thyroxine-binding globulin is increased by exogenous oestrogens and pregnancy.

49. **A B C D**

Progesterone is able to promote the excretion of sodium, probably by antagonising the action of aldosterone on the distal renal tubule. Progesterone acts on secondary sexual organs only when they have been prepared by the action of oestrogens. Progesterone is formed in the ovary, placenta, adrenal gland and testis in man. It is a relaxant of smooth muscle in blood vessels, uterus and alimentary tract and possibly ureter. Arrhenoblastomas are usually androgen secreting tumours; tumours more likely to produce progesterone are luteal cell tumours and teratomas/chorionepitheliomas and occasionally granulosa cell tumours.

50. A C D E

Metastases are characteristic of malignancy. Malignant tumours tend to have a rapid rate of growth, but some grow more slowly than adjacent normal tissue (for example, some gut carcinomas). The presence of mitotic figures, particularly abnormal forms, is characteristic of malignancy. Malignant tumours tend to invade surrounding tissues (carcinoma of the cervix is a good example). Loss of differentiation may be a feature of malignant tumours but a number of malignancies are characterised by well-differentiated tissue (for example, the mucus-secreting glands of well-differentiated adenocarcinoma of the cervix).

51. B D E

Physiological jaundice in a healthy baby appears after the first 48 hours of life, reaches a peak by about the fourth day and disappears within 7-10 days. The bowel is usually sterile at birth but is rapidly colonised by organisms including those encountered along the birth canal and perineum. Urine is seen to be passed in utero on ultrasound and is frequently passed at or soon after birth. The respiratory rate is usually less than 60 per minute at rest, 25-35 being usual. Constriction of the ductus arteriosus is brought about by the direct effect on the vessel wall of raising the arteriolar pO_2 with ventilation of the lungs at birth. There is probably a rapid partial closure soon after birth followed by a more gradual closure during the course of several days.

52. A B D

Phaeochromocytoma is a rare cause of hypertension. Tumours arising in the adrenal medulla usually secrete both noradrenaline and adrenaline while those originating in extra-adrenal chromaffin tissue secrete chiefly noradrenaline. Over 90% of tumours are benign. The greatest incidence is seen in the third and fourth decades. Although paroxysmal or sustained hypertension is the most common presentation, a small number of patients display profound paroxysmal hypotension and tachycardia or alternating hypotension and hypertension.

53. **A B D**

The superior surface of the sphenoid bone is indented to form the pituitary fossa (sella turcica); anterior is the shallow optic groove in which the optic nerves run. The optic chiasma is superior and posterior to the stalk; thus a tumour of the gland usually passes in front of the chiasma pressing on the medial sides of the optic nerves causing hemianopia of temporal fields. The two cavernous sinuses lie on either side. The pituitary gland receives its blood supply from the internal carotid artery and vessels in the tuber cinereum. The gland is all ectodermal in origin; Rathke's pouch (a midline ectodermal diverticulum from the stomodeum) forms the anterior lobe and the posterior lobe develops as a diverticulum from the floor of the diencephalon.

54. **A D**

Our understanding of the changes in cardiac output in pregnancy have evolved gradually with changes in measurement techniques. The most widely accepted view is that in the normal pregnant woman at rest, not lying supine, cardiac output rises from early pregnancy to a peak at around 20 weeks gestation which is approximately 1.5 litres per minute of 40% above the non-pregnant level; this level seems to be maintained throughout the rest of pregnancy, although venous pressure in the legs has been shown to increase during pregnancy, that in the arms is unaltered, and central venous pressure is said to remain in the range 2-5 cm of water. Peripheral resistance is calculated from the mean arterial pressure divided by cardiac output; since cardiac output is increased, and arterial blood pressure if anything falls slightly, it follows that peripheral resistance must be decreased. The fall has been estimated at between 20 and 40%, and seems to be maximal in mid-pregnancy; this is due to the opening up of new vascular beds within the uterus and placenta, and a general relaxation in peripheral vascular tone. The increased cardiac output of pregnancy is achieved by both an increase in heart rate (averaging 15 beats/min) and stroke volume (from 65 to 70 ml); again these changes are present from early pregnancy.

55. A E

Anatomically the ribs flare out in pregnancy long before there is any mechanical pressure; the subcostal angle changes from 68 degrees to 80 degrees by the 20th week. The diaphragm is raised and its excursion with respiration is greater. Airways resistance is reduced. The tidal volume, the volume inspired and exhaled at each breath, increases progressively throughout pregnancy and thus increases the minute ventilation as the respiratory rate remains unchanged. The vital capacity, the maximum volume of air that can be forcibly inspired after a maximum expiration, is probably unchanged although it has been suggested that there may be a slight increase (2% during the whole of pregnancy). Overall the total lung capacity is increased marginally.

56. C

The agent responsible is a double-stranded DNA virus. The primary attack has a much shorter incubation period of less than one week. HSV type 2 is more likely to cause earlier and more frequent recurrences than HSV type 1, which in fact is more likely to cause labial rather than genital herpes. Zidovudine has been found to be of benefit in HIV infection. It is the antiviral agent acyclovir which is used in the management of genital herpes.

57. D

Fibrinogen is synthesised in the liver and is responsible for blood coagulation. The concentration in plasma is markedly increased in pregnancy. The normal non-pregnant levels are in the region of 250-400 mg/100 ml in late pregnancy. The conversion of soluble plasma protein fibrinogen to insoluble fibrin is catalysed by thrombin. Vitamin K is necessary for prothrombin production. Vitamin K is necessary for prothrombin production; coumarin derivatives competitively inhibit vitamin K.

58. A D E

A normal diet would provide 12-15 mg iron daily. Ferric iron is not absorbed and must be reduced to the ferrous form before passing the gut wall; this reduction is assisted by ascorbic acid and sulphur-containing amino acids. Iron absorption is normally 10-15% but is increased if the body stores are reduced or the rate of formation of red cells is increased.

59. A B D E

The overall effect of aldosterone is to increase the amount of sodium in the body, its main action being to increase sodium absorption from the distal renal tubule and from the ascending limb of the loop of Henle and collecting ducts in exchange for potassium and hydrogen ions. Sodium retention is accompanied by water retention, increasing the extracellular fluid volume, and therefore total weight, serum chloride level rises, in parallel with the sodium level.

60. D E

Fatty acids and monoglycerides are not water soluble; bile salts convert them to micelles, particles less than 0.5 micrometres in diameter. Chylomicrons consist of cholesterol, phospholipid and protein and are the forms in which lipids accumulating in the cells pass out into the lymph. Dietary fat is absorbed in the upper part of the small intestine. The rate of cholesterol and myelin lipids synthesis is low in adult central nervous system. Fatty acids on oxidation yield a large quantity of energy. Linoleic acid is an essential fatty acid.

MCQ REVISION INDEX

Each item below refers to a specific page number, not to a question number.

PasTest has over 25 years of experience in helping people pass first time, with specially tailored courses to make the most of your valuable revision time.

Our lecturers are highly qualified, practicing doctors from leading teaching hospitals. Professor John Lumley of St Bartholomews Hospital, London, is the Senior Advisor for our surgical courses and has been closely involved in their development.

PasTest know what it takes to help you pass. To give you the best chance we

- select only the best lecturers in the field (and we continually assess their performance).

- use teaching methods which are stimulating and make learning more enjoyable.

- provide you with a comprehensive course binder including essential MCQs and EMQs which cover the entire MRCS syllabus and allow you to assess your knowledge.

- give you invaluable tips on exam preparation and presentation.

Consolidate your learning with a PasTest revision course, call now for details:

Freephone 0800 980 9814

PasTest, Freepost, Knutsford, Cheshire, WA16 7BR. Fax: 01565 650264
E-mail: enquiries@pastest.co.uk http://www.pastest.co.uk

NOTES

NOTES

NOTES

NOTES